# DISCOVERING MATHEMATICS 2B

## Workbook

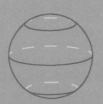

Victor Chow

OXFORD
UNIVERSITY PRESS

# HOW TO USE THIS BOOK

This write-in Workbook is for use with *Discovering Mathematics* **Student Book 2B**.
It can be used for extra practice in class or as homework activities.

- **Exercises are written for each chapter section,** while **Review Exercises** test your ability to apply concepts and techniques across a group of chapters.

- Each exercise is split into **three levels**:
  **Level 1:** simple questions to practise your understanding of concepts
  **Level 2:** harder questions which involve direct application
  **Level 3:** hardest questions, with a focus on problem solving

- For some questions, **hints are given** to help you.

- Watch for the different icons next to questions:

   and  highlight the content related to other subjects

   shows where more than one answer is possible

  identifies where you can practise your problem-solving skills

- You are told in the question if you should or shouldn't use a **calculator**. If there is no instruction, you can decide for yourself or ask your teacher.

- Your teacher can access the answers for you from two places:
  **Short answers** are available free (and password protected) at www.oxfordsecondary.co.uk/discoveringmathematics-answers
  **Fully-worked solutions** are on Kerboodle

- Use the **progress tracker** at the start to log your progress and to note where you might need some support as you work through each section.

---

# OXFORD
## UNIVERSITY PRESS

Great Clarendon Street, Oxford, OX2 6DP, United Kingdom

Oxford University Press is a department of the University of Oxford. It furthers the University's objective of excellence in research, scholarship, and education by publishing worldwide. Oxford is a registered trade mark of Oxford University Press in the UK and in certain other countries

British Library Cataloguing in Publication Data
Data available

978-0-19-842195-5

1 3 5 7 9 10 8 6 4 2

Paper used in the production of this book is a natural, recyclable product made from wood grown in sustainable forests. The manufacturing process conforms to the environmental regulations of the country of origin.

Printed and Bound by CPI Group (UK) Ltd, Croydon, CR0 4YY

**Acknowledgements**
The author and publishers would like to thank the reviewer team of **consultants** – Simon d'Angelo, Liz Henning, Ann Lui, Sian Thomas – and **teachers** – Pippa Baker, Jill Borcherds, Lana Laidler, Jo Walker – who have advised on the content of this book. Their contributions have been invaluable.

Editorial team: Dom Holdsworth, Julie Thornton, Rosie Day, Sarah Dutton, Isobel Fray, Emma Gadsden and Matteo Orsini Jones. With thanks also to Katie Wood for her contributions.

The publishers would also like to thank the following for permissions to use copyright material:

**Cover:** Matt Anderson Photography/Getty Images

**Photos: p21:** oversnap/iStock; **p27:** Mega Pixel/Shutterstock; **p31:** StudioSmart/Shutterstock; **p38 (L):** Gemenacom/Shutterstock; **p38 (R):** Gemenacom/Shutterstock; **p50:** bumihills/Shutterstock; **p100:** Yuliyan Velchev/Shutterstock; **p112:** Papriko/Shutterstock; **p122 (L):** johavel/ Shutterstock; **p122 (R):** Kolonko/Shutterstock; **p124:** Africa Studio/ Shutterstock; **p127:** Taku/Shutterstock; **p130:** Suwichan/Shutterstock; **p133:** tratong/Shutterstock; **p151:** Gino Santa Maria/Shutterstock; **p153:** Malyugin/Shutterstock; **p155:** Quang Ho/Shutterstock

**Data: p137, p139 (B):** Office for National Statistics; **p140 (T):** ukpublicspending.co.uk; **p143, p152 (B):** Office for National Statistics

Although we have made every effort to trace and contact all copyright holders before publication this has not been possible in all cases. If notified, the publisher will rectify any errors or omissions at the earliest opportunity.

Links to third party websites are provided by Oxford in good faith and for information only. Oxford disclaims any responsibility for the materials contained in any third party website referenced in this work.

# CONTENTS

# TRACK YOUR PROGRESS

Tick your progress in the boxes below and use the space to write a reminder about your learning.

# Factors and Multiples

## 1.1 Primes, Prime Factorisation and Index Notation

**LEVEL 1**

1.  Write down the positive factors of each number and state whether or not the number is a prime.

    **(a)** 45

    $45 = 1 \times 45$

    $\quad = 3 \times \underline{\hspace{1.5cm}}$

    $\quad = \underline{\hspace{1.5cm}}$

    The positive factors of 45 are:

    _____

    45 <u>is</u> / <u>is not</u> a prime number.

    **(b)** 37

2.  **(a)** Find the largest multiple of 7 which is less than 200.

    **(b)** Find the smallest multiple of 9 which is greater than 300.

3.  Find the prime factors of each number and hence write each number as a product of its prime factors in index notation.

    **(a)** 48

    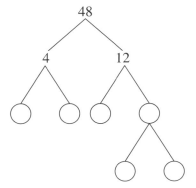

    **(b)** 150

4. Determine whether each statement is true or false. For any statement that is false, give an example to show that it is false.

   (a) If 10 is a factor of a number, then 5 is a factor of the number.

   (b) If 3 and 9 are factors of a number, then 27 is a factor of the number.

   (c) If 2 and 11 are factors of a number, then 22 is a factor of the number.

5. (a) Complete the factor tree.

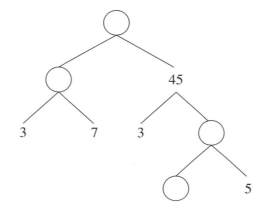

   (b) Express the number at the top of the factor tree as a product of its prime factors in index notation.

6. Express each expression as a single number in index notation.

   (a) $7^3 \times 7^2$                    (b) $4^6 \div 4^2$

   (c) $(3^2)^4$                      (d) $(5^3)^6$

**PROBLEM SOLVING** **7.** A leap year has one extra day, 29 February. Between the years 2000 and 2100, a leap year occurs every four years.

2012 and 2016 are leap years.

**(a)** Write down the next three leap years after 2016.

**(b)** What is the common property of these leap years?

**8.** It is given that $p$ is a prime number greater than 2.

**(a)** Explain why $p + 3$ cannot be a prime number.

**(b)** Can $p + 2$ be a prime number? Explain your answer.

**OPEN QUESTION** **9.** Two numbers can be expressed as

$$5^2 \times 7^3 \times 17 \times 19^2 \quad \text{and} \quad 5^3 \times 7 \times 11^3 \times 19.$$

Write down three common factors of these two numbers in index notation.

# 1.2 Highest Common Factor (HCF)

## ⚙ LEVEL 1

1. **(a)** Find the positive factors of 35.

   **(b)** Find the positive factors of 56.

   **(c)** List the common positive factors of 35 and 56 and hence write down their HCF.

2. Express each number as a product of its prime factors and hence find the HCF of each pair of numbers.
   **(a)** 40 and 48

   **(b)** 66 and 99

   **(c)** 105 and 225

   **(d)** 135 and 315

**3.** Find the HCF of each group of numbers.
   **(a)** 16, 64 and 72

   **(b)** 35, 54 and 90

   **(c)** 260, 325 and 455

**4.** Find the HCF of each group of numbers.
   **(a)** $2^3 \times 3^2 \times 5$ and $2^2 \times 3 \times 5^2$

   **(b)** $3^4 \times 7^2 \times 11$ and $3^3 \times 7^5 \times 13$

   **(c)** $2^4 \times 3^2 \times 5$, $2^3 \times 3^3 \times 5^2$ and $2^2 \times 3^5 \times 5^3$

   **(d)** $5^2 \times 7^3 \times 11$, $5 \times 7^4 \times 19^2$ and $2^3 \times 3^2 \times 19^3$

5. A rectangular sheet of paper is 63 cm by 54 cm. It is divided into a grid of squares. What is the greatest possible length of a side of each square?

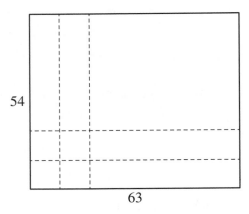

6. As part of a promotion, a company has 420 pens and 504 keyrings to be distributed equally among its customer organisations. What is the greatest number of organisations that will receive the promotional items?

7. There are 405 green, 360 red and 195 white plates. Plates of each colour are put into stacks with an equal number of plates in each stack. Find the greatest number of plates in a stack.

8. Find the largest number that divides into 407, 497 and 722, and leaves the same remainder, 2, in each case.

# 1.3  Lowest Common Multiple (LCM)

## ⚙ LEVEL 1

1.  **(a)** List the first ten positive multiples of 8.

    **(b)** List the first ten positive multiples of 12.

    **(c)** Write down the LCM of 8 and 12.

2.  Express each number as a product of its prime factors and hence find the LCM of each pair of numbers.
    **(a)** 30 and 42

    **(b)** 4 and 17

    **(c)** 50 and 75

    **(d)** 66 and 528

    **(e)** 52 and 117

3. Find the LCM of each group of numbers.
   (a) 4, 6 and 21

   (b) 8, 12 and 15

   (c) 4, 7 and 11

4. Two numbers are
   $3^2 \times 5^3 \times 7 \times 11^4$ and $3^3 \times 5 \times 7^2 \times 11^3$.
   (a) Find the HCF of these two numbers. Give your answer as a product of prime factors in index notation.

   (b) Find the LCM of these two numbers. Give your answer as a product of prime factors in index notation.

5. The HCF of two numbers is 16. The LCM of these two numbers is 3600. If one number is 144, find the other number.

 **LEVEL 3**

6. Heidi goes to a market at 10 am every 8 days. Pablo goes to the market at 10 am every 14 days. One day they meet each other at the market. After how many days will they meet again at the market?

7. A row of square tiles of side 30 cm and a row of square tiles of side 55 cm have the same length.
   (a) What is the minimum length of each row?

   (b) Find the number of tiles of side 30 cm in the row in (a).

 **PROBLEM SOLVING**

8. A crate of oranges can be exactly divided into bags of 5, 9 or 12 oranges. Find the smallest number of oranges in the crate.

**PROBLEM SOLVING**

9. When a number is divided by 6, 7 or 8, it leaves a remainder of 5. The number is divisible by 11. Find the smallest possible value of the number.

# 1.4 Square Roots, Cube Roots and Prime Factorisation

 **LEVEL 1**

1. Find the length of a side of a square with the given area, without using a calculator.
   (a)  49 cm$^2$                    (b)  625 cm$^2$

2. Find these values without using a calculator.
   (a)  $\sqrt{484}$                  (b)  $\sqrt{729}$

3. Find the length of a side of a cube with the given volume, without using a calculator.
   (a)  64 cm$^3$                     (b)  5832 cm$^3$

4. Find these values using prime factorisation.
   (a)  $\sqrt[3]{2744}$              (b)  $\sqrt[3]{9261}$

**5.** Find the positive square roots of these numbers. Leave your answers in index notation.

    **(a)** $2^6 \times 5^2$                                 **(b)** $3^8 \times 7^4$

**6.** Find the cube roots of these numbers. Leave your answers in index notation.

    **(a)** $3^6 \times 11^3$                               **(b)** $5^9 \times 13^{12}$

**7.**   **(a)** Find the cube of $3^4 \times 7^2$, leaving your answer in index notation.

    **(b)** Find the positive square root of the result in **(a)**, leaving your answer in index notation.

**8.**   **(a)** Find the square of $11^3 \times 13^6$, leaving your answer in index notation.

    **(b)** Find the cube root of the result in **(a)**, leaving your answer in index notation.

9. The area of a face of a cubical glass paperweight is $196\,cm^2$. Calculate
   (a) the length of an edge of the cube,

   (b) the volume of the cube.

10. (a) Express $291\,600$ as a product of its prime factors in index notation.

    (b) The length of a supporting beam is $\sqrt{291\,600}\,cm$. Work out the length in metres.

11. (a) Express $343\,000$ as a product of its prime factors in index notation.

    (b) The height of a cylinder is $\sqrt[3]{343\,000}$ cm. Work out the height in metres.

# Approximation and Estimation

## 2.1 Rounding Numbers to Decimal Places

### ⚙ LEVEL 1

1. Round these numbers to the nearest integer.
   (a) 25.6
   = _____ (to the nearest integer)
   (b) 329.18

2. Round these numbers to the nearest 100.
   (a) 48 235
   (b) −2863.07

3. Round these numbers to one decimal place.
   (a) 41.32
   (b) 28.953

   (c) −0.471
   (d) 234.98

4. Round these numbers to two decimal places.
   (a) 8.471
   (b) 29.3576

5. Round these numbers to three decimal places.
   (a) 25.9203
   (b) −417.5045

6. Round these numbers to four decimal places.
   (a) −4.050 307
   (b) 6.398 25

 **LEVEL 2**

**7.**   **(a)**   Calculate $-26 \times [-15 - (-11)]$.

      **(b)**   Round the answer in **(a)** to the nearest 10.

**8.**   **(a)**   Evaluate $23.48 + 3.79 - 65.84$.

      **(b)**   Round the answer in **(a)** to one decimal place.

**9.**   Express these fractions as decimals to three decimal places.

    **(a)**   $-\dfrac{5}{6}$                           **(b)**   $\dfrac{3}{11}$

**10.**   Evaluate these expressions and give the answers as decimals to two decimal places.

    **(a)**   $1\dfrac{3}{7} \times 2\dfrac{1}{2}$                       **(b)**   $2\dfrac{1}{3} \div 4\dfrac{1}{5}$

11. The mid-year estimate of the UK population in 2015 was 65 110 000. The estimate in 2016 was 65 648 100.
    (a) Round the estimate in 2016 to the nearest million.

    (b) Find the increase in the estimated mid-year population from 2015 to 2016.

    (c) Round the answer in (b) to the nearest 10 000.

12. In the Commonwealth Youth Games 2017, Holly Mills of England won the gold medal in the Girls Long Jump event with a distance of 6.19 m. Tatiana Aholou of Canada won the silver medal with a distance of 5.97 m.
    (a) Round the distance that Holly Mills jumped to the nearest metre.

    (b) Find the difference between the distances jumped by Holly Mills and Tatiana Aholou, giving your answer to one decimal place.

13. The mass of each piece of synthetic diamond is 0.2063 grams.
    (a) Round the mass to three decimal places.

    (b) Find the total mass of eight pieces of the diamond, giving your answer to two decimal places.

## 2.2 Rounding Numbers to Significant Figures

### ⚙ LEVEL 1

**1.** Round each number to two significant figures.
   **(a)** 14.53
       = _____ (to 2 sf)

   **(b)** 234.71

   **(c)** 2.905

   **(d)** −0.3210

**2.** Round each number to three significant figures.
   **(a)** 63 271

   **(b)** −26.025

   **(c)** 1.0706

   **(d)** 0.003 795

**3.** Round each number to four significant figures.
   **(a)** 432 713

   **(b)** 2345.681

   **(c)** −63.2498

   **(d)** 0.070 0962

**4.** State the number of significant figures in each number.
   **(a)** 0.403

   **(b)** 0.4030

   **(c)** 34 509

   **(d)** 34 500

   **(e)** 0.036 091

   **(f)** 0.036 090

5. **(a)** Calculate $-4.769 + 1.875 \times 9$.

**(b)** Round the answer in **(a)** to two significant figures.

6. **(a)** Convert $2\dfrac{5}{18}$ into a decimal using a written method.

**(b)** Round the answer in **(a)** to four significant figures.

7. **(a)** Evaluate $3\dfrac{2}{5} + \left(-2\dfrac{4}{5}\right) \div 1\dfrac{3}{8}$.

**(b)** Express the answer in **(a)** as a decimal, rounded to three significant figures.

8. Consider the two numbers 3.042 and 3.0420.
   **(a)** Are the values of these two numbers equal?

   **(b)** Are the degrees of accuracy of these two numbers the same? Explain your answer.

**9.** The number of overseas visitors to the UK in June 2017 was 3555 thousand.

   **(a)** How many significant figures are there in this number?

   **(b)** Write the number 3555 thousand in full, rounded to three significant figures.

   **(c)** The number of overseas visitors to the UK in July 2017 was 465 thousand more than that in June. Find the number of overseas visitors in July 2017, giving the answer to two significant figures.

 **10.** The mass of $7 \text{ cm}^3$ of copper is 62.72 grams.

   **(a)** Find the mass of $1 \text{ cm}^3$ of copper.

   **(b)** Round your answer in **(a)** to two significant figures.

**11.** The length of a room is 12.3 m. The width of the room is 7.06 m.

   **(a)** Work out the perimeter of the room, giving your answer to three significant figures.

   **(b)** Work out the area of the room and round your answer to four significant figures.

## 2.3 Estimation

1. Without using a calculator, estimate the value of each expression by rounding each number in the expression to one significant figure.
   (a)  4389 + 5261
   (b)  7813 ÷ 22.9

   (c)  365 − 4.82 × 19.1
   (d)  (82.9 − 45.3) ÷ 4.07

2. State, giving reasons, whether each estimate on the right-hand side is a reasonable approximation to the value of the expression on the left-hand side.
   (a)  478 − 237 + 619 ≈ 900

   (b)  25.23 × 5.92 ≈ 150

3. Work out the value of each expression using a calculator and round your answer to one significant figure.
   (a)  6257 × 0.308
   (b)  (23.46 − 9.87) ÷ 0.053

4. State the possible range of the actual value of each quantity, in the form $a \le x < b$.
   (a)  time = 20 min, to 1 sf

   (b)  depth = 460 mm, to 2 sf

**LEVEL 2**

5.  Estimate the values of these expressions.
    (a)  $\sqrt{223}$

    (b)  $\sqrt[3]{219}$

    (c)  $(17.42 - 23.58) \times \sqrt{396}$

    (d)  $0.309 \div \sqrt[3]{27.1}$

6.  Consider the expression $24.476 - 17.849 + 45.417$.
    (a)  Work out the value of the expression, giving your answer to three significant figures.

    (b)  Round each number in the expression to three significant figures and then evaluate the expression.

    (c)  Are the answers in (a) and (b) the same? Which is more accurate? Give your reason.

7.  The price of a T-shirt is £10, accurate to one significant figure. The price of a jacket is £40, accurate to one significant figure. Find the range, in the form $a \leq x < b$, of the possible total price of
    (a)  three T-shirts,

    (b)  three T-shirts and one jacket.

**8.** The photo shows a black cab and a double-decker bus.

It is known that a black cab is 1.77 m high. Estimate the height of the bus.

**9.** The thickness of a £1 coin is 2.80 mm. The thickness of a £2 coin is 2.50 mm.

**(a)** A stack of coins has seven £1 coins and six £2 coins.

    **(i)** Calculate the height of the stack.

    **(ii)** Round the answer in **(i)** to one significant figure.

**(b)** Find the LCM of 280 and 250.

**(c)** A stack of £1 coins and a stack of £2 coins have equal height. Work out the minimum number of £1 coins in the stack.

# 3 Ratio, Rate and Speed

## 3.1 Integer Ratios

⚙ **LEVEL 1**

1. Simplify these ratios.
   **(a)** 16 : 20

   **(b)** 45 : 25

   **(c)** 56 cm : 42 cm

   **(d)** 2 hours : 40 minutes

2. Throughout her career, an athlete won six gold medals and four silver medals. Find
   **(a)** the ratio of the number of gold medals to the number of silver medals in its simplest form,

   **(b)** the number of silver medals as a fraction of the total number of medals.

3. The ratio of the price of a cake to the price of a tart is 5 : 4. If the price of the tart is £12, find the price of the cake.

4. A company has 72 members of staff. The ratio of the number of part-time staff to the number of full-time staff is 3 : 5. Find the number of part-time staff.

**5.** In a large floral display, the ratio of red flowers to yellow flowers is $4:7$. The number of red flowers is 12 less than the number of yellow flowers. Calculate the combined total number of red and yellow flowers in the display.

**6.** A recipe for salad dressing requires vinegar and oil in the ratio $1:5$ by volume. 200 ml of oil is used to make some salad dressing according to this recipe. Find the total volume of the salad dressing made.

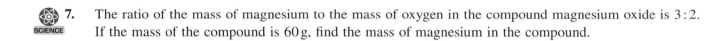

**SCIENCE**

**7.** The ratio of the mass of magnesium to the mass of oxygen in the compound magnesium oxide is $3:2$. If the mass of the compound is 60 g, find the mass of magnesium in the compound.

**8.** After a day's trading at a craft fair, the ratio of the number of £5 notes to the number of £20 notes in a stallholder's takings is $11:3$. The total value of the notes is £345. Work out the number of £5 notes.

**PROBLEM SOLVING** **9.** The ratio of the width to the height of a rectangular computer monitor is 16 : 9. The perimeter of the monitor is 150 cm. Calculate
   **(a)** the width of the monitor,



   **(b)** the area of the monitor.




**PROBLEM SOLVING** **10.** The ratio of Ahmed's age to Belinda's age is 3 : 5. In four years' time, the ratio of their ages will become 2 : 3. Find Ahmed's present age.




**PROBLEM SOLVING** **11.** The ratio of the height of a runner bean plant to the height of a pea plant is 3 : 4. When the height of the runner bean plant increases by 25 cm and the height of the pea plant remains unchanged, the ratio of their heights will become 7 : 6. Find the height of the pea plant.

✓ **Track your progress in the checklist on page iv.**

## 3.2 All Kinds of Ratios

**1.** Express each ratio in its simplest form.

    **(a)** $1 : \dfrac{2}{3}$

    **(b)** $2\dfrac{1}{4} : 3\dfrac{3}{8}$

    **(c)** $0.28 : 0.49$

    **(d)** $1.25 : 0.75$

**2.** Express each ratio in its simplest form.

    **(a)** $0.4 : \dfrac{7}{20}$

    **(b)** $1\dfrac{1}{3} : 0.12$

    **(c)** $60\,\text{cm} : 4.5\,\text{m}$

    **(d)** $3\dfrac{3}{4}$ hours : 25 minutes

**3.** At a scenic spot, two walking trails are signposted. The Beach Trail is 850 m long and the Hillside Trail is $3\dfrac{2}{25}$ km long. Find the ratio of the length of the Hillside Trail to the length of the Beach Trail.

**4.** In an examination, the time allowed for paper I is 1 hour and the time allowed for paper II is $1\dfrac{1}{2}$ hours. Find

    **(a)** the ratio of the time allowed for paper II to the time allowed for paper I,

    **(b)** the ratio of the time allowed for paper II to the total time allowed for both papers.

**5.** Given that $3a = 4b$, determine
    **(a)** $a:b$,
    **(b)** $a^2:b^2$.

**6.** Simplify these ratios.
    **(a)** $a:b:c = 8:22:14$
    **(b)** $g:h:k = 6:3:1\frac{5}{7}$

    **(c)** $p:q:r = 2\frac{2}{3}:3\frac{1}{5}:1\frac{1}{15}$
    **(d)** $x:y:z = 2.1:3.5:14$

**7.** The lengths of the edges of three cubes A, B and C are 12 cm, 15 cm and 21 cm respectively. Find the ratio, in the simplest form, of
    **(a)** the edges of the cubes,

    **(b)** the surface areas of the cubes,

    **(c)** the volumes of the cubes.

**8.** An award of £750 is shared between two business partners, Jamie and Maria, in the ratio $0.42:0.48$. How much does Maria get?

**9.** Find $a:b:c$ in each case. The ratio should be in its simplest form.

    **(a)** $a:b = 3:2$ and $b:c = 6:5$

    **(b)** $a:b = 0.63:0.81$ and $b:c = 1:\dfrac{1}{6}$

**10.** In a tool box, the ratio of the number of bolts to the number of nuts is $5:3$, and the ratio of the number of bolts to the number of washers is $6:5$.

    **(a)** Calculate the ratio bolts : nuts : washers.

Bolt

Washer

Nut

    **(b)** There is a total of 146 bolts, nuts and washers in the tool box. Find the number of bolts.

**11.** In a fridge, the numbers of tomatoes, apricots and peaches are in the ratio $4:5:6$. There are 24 peaches. Find

    **(a)** the number of apricots,

    **(b)** the total number of these fruits.

## 3.3 Scale Plans and Maps

### ⚙ LEVEL 1

1. Express each map scale in the form $1:r$.
   (a) $1\,\text{cm}:6\,\text{m}$

   (b) $2\,\text{cm}:400\,\text{m}$

   (c) $3\,\text{cm}:12\,\text{km}$

   (d) $5\,\text{cm}:12\,\text{km}$

2. Find the value of $x$ in each case.
   (a) $1:300 = 1\,\text{cm}:x\,\text{m}$

   (b) $1:2000 = 1\,\text{cm}:x\,\text{m}$

   (c) $1:50\,000 = 1\,\text{cm}:x\,\text{km}$

   (d) $1:200\,000 = 1\,\text{cm}:x\,\text{km}$

3. The scale of a town centre map is $1:4000$. A road is $5\,\text{cm}$ long on the map. Find the actual length of the road in metres.

4. The scale of a map is $1:20\,000$. A river is $3\,\text{km}$ long. Find the length of the river on the map in cm.

5.  In a scale drawing of a car, the car's length of 5 m is represented by 25 cm.
    **(a)** Express the scale of the drawing in the form $1:r$.

    **(b)** Find the distance on the drawing, in cm, that represents the car's width of 1.8 m.

6.  An actual distance of 5 km is represented by a distance of 4 cm on a map.
    **(a)** Express the scale of the map in the form $1:r$.

    **(b)** The distance between two cinemas on the map is 6 cm. Find the actual distance between the cinemas in km.

7.  The scale of a map is $1:4000$.
    **(a)** Find the actual area, in $m^2$, of a school if its area on the map is 25 cm$^2$.

    **(b)** Find the area, in cm$^2$, of a garden on the map if its actual area is 24 000 m$^2$.

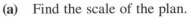
8. A scale floor plan of a flat is shown. On the plan,
   $AG = 5.0\,cm$, $BC = 2.0\,cm$ and $CD = 2.7\,cm$.
   The actual length of the wall $AG$ is 7.0 m.
   **(a)** Find the scale of the plan.

   **(b)** Work out the actual length of $BC$ in m.

   **(c)** Work out the actual area of the bedroom $BCDE$.

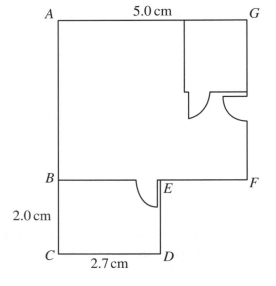

9. The map of the River Thames in London shows the relative locations of three tourist attractions. It is drawn to the scale shown.

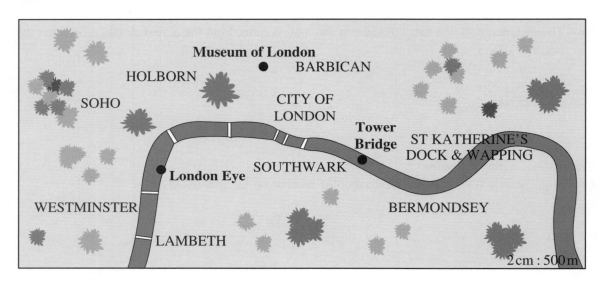

   **(a)** Express the scale of the map in the form $1 : r$.

   **(b)** Using the map, estimate the actual direct distance, in metres to the nearest 100 metres, between
   **(i)** the Museum of London and Tower Bridge,

   **(ii)** the London Eye and Tower Bridge.

## 3.4 Rate

### ⚙ LEVEL 1

1.  Find the rate in each case.
    (a) The cost of 3 kg of chicken is £15.
        The price rate of chicken is £ _____ /kg.

    (b) A carpenter makes 16 cupboard doors in 8 hours.
        This production rate is _____ cupboard doors/hour.

    (c) The annual rent of a flat is £15 000.
        The rate of rent is £ _____ /month.

    (d) The mass of 9 m of a metal bar is 13.5 kg.
        The rate of the mass of the bar is _____ kg/m.

2.  There are eight flapjacks in each packet. The price for three packets is £12. Find the price rate of flapjacks in
    (a) £ per packet,

    (b) £ per flapjack.

3.  The total mass of 12 iron balls is 936 grams. The volume of each ball is 10 cm$^3$. Find
    (a) the mass of iron per ball,

    (b) the mass of iron per cm$^3$.

4.  A hall has six sets of pendant lights. Each set has five identical bulbs.
    The total power consumption of these lights is 240 watts. Calculate
    (a) the power consumption per set,

    (b) the power consumption per bulb.

**5.** The price for six packs of printing paper is £45.
   **(a)** Work out the price per pack.

   **(b)** What is the price for eight packs?

**6.** A technician charges £115 for a five-hour job. The charge is based only on her time.
   **(a)** Find her charge per hour.

   **(b)** What would be her charge for a four-hour job?

**7.** A sunblock lotion is sold in two different sizes as shown. Which size gives the better value? Explain your answer.

 Regular size
200ml £5.00

 Family size
350ml £8.40

**8.** A car consumes 12 litres of petrol on a journey of 200 km.

   **(a)** Find its petrol consumption rate in

      **(i)** km/litre,

      **(ii)** litres/100 km.

   **(b)** If the car has 54 litres of petrol, how far would you expect it to travel?

**9.** A silver plate has a mass of 210 g and a volume of $20 \text{ cm}^3$.

   **(a)** Find the density (that is, the mass per $\text{cm}^3$) of silver.

   **(b)** A rectangular silver bar is 8 cm long, 3 cm wide and 2 cm high. Find the mass of this bar.

**10.** On 13 May 2018, the exchange rate between the euro (EUR) and the British pound (GBP) was 1 EUR = 0.8818 GBP. The exchange rate between the British pound and the US dollar (USD) was 1 GBP = 1.354 USD.

   **(a)** A camera was for sale at 400 EUR on a French website. Find its price in pounds to the nearest pound.

   **(b)** The same model of camera was for sale at 450 USD on a US website. Find its price in pounds to the nearest pound.

   **(c)** A customer in the UK wants to buy this camera. Which site's price is better? Explain your answer.

# 3.5 Speed

 **1.** Ruby hummingbirds migrate from Mexico to Florida in spring. They fly a non-stop 800 km journey across the Gulf of Mexico in 20 hours. Find the average speed of the birds on their migration.

**2.** Complete the table.

|     | Distance travelled | Time taken | Average speed |
| --- | --- | --- | --- |
| **(a)** | 165 km | 3 h | km/h |
| **(b)** | 400 m | 80 s | m/s |
| **(c)** |  | 2 h | 73 km/h |
| **(d)** |  | 9 s | 6 m/s |
| **(e)** | 72 km |  | 48 km/h |
| **(f)** | 84 m |  | 7 m/s |

**3.** Convert these speeds to m/s.
    **(a)** 36 km/h                     **(b)** 48 km/h

    **(c)** 81 km/h                     **(d)** 120 km/h

**4.** Convert these speeds to km/h.
    **(a)** 4 m/s                      **(b)** 11 m/s

    **(c)** 15 m/s                      **(d)** 30 m/s

5. A girl runs at a constant speed of 8 m/s.
   (a) Calculate the time, in seconds, she takes to run 100 m.

   (b) Find the distance she covers in 1 minute 10 seconds.

6. A minibus travelled for 8 hours 42 minutes. Its average speed was 54 km/h.
   (a) Express 8 hours 42 minutes in hours as a decimal.

   (b) Find the distance that the minibus travelled to the nearest km.

7. A high-speed train travels 160 km in 40 minutes.
   (a) Find its average speed in km/h.

   (b) At this average speed, how many hours would the train take to travel 300 km?

8. Dan takes 25 seconds to swim 50 m.
   (a) Find his average speed for this distance.

   (b) If his average speed for 100 m is 0.125 m/s less than that for 50 m, find the time he takes to swim 100 m. Round your answer to two decimal places.

**SCIENCE**

**9.** The flight route from Hong Kong to London Heathrow Airport is 9648 km. The flight time of a plane is 12 hours.

  **(a)** Find the average speed of the plane in km/h.

  **(b)** The local time of Hong Kong is 8 hours ahead of the local time of London. If the plane departs Hong Kong at 9.05 am, what is the local time when it arrives in London?

Hong Kong    London

**PROBLEM SOLVING**

**10.** A car is driven at 60 km/h along city roads for half an hour. It is then driven 135 km along a motorway at 90 km/h. Find the average speed of the car for the whole journey in km/h.

**PROBLEM SOLVING**

**11.** In a 100 m race at Sports Day, Adam's time is 12 seconds and Brendan's time is 12.5 seconds.

  **(a)** Find the average speeds of Adam and Brendan in the race.

  **(b)** When Adam reaches the finishing line, by how many metres is Brendan behind him?

  **(c)** What assumption did you make in working out part **(b)**?

✓ **Track your progress in the checklist on page iv.**

# 4 More Percentages

## 4.1 Expressing a Percentage as a Fraction or a Decimal

**LEVEL 1**

1. Express each fraction as a percentage.
   (a) $\frac{3}{5} = \frac{3}{5} \times 100\%$
       $= \underline{\hspace{2em}}$

   (b) $\frac{8}{25}$

   (c) $2\frac{3}{8}$

   (d) $3\frac{5}{6}$

2. Express each percentage as a fraction in its simplest form.
   (a) $68\% = \frac{68}{100}$
       $= \underline{\hspace{2em}}$

   (b) $150\%$

   (c) $37\frac{1}{2}\%$

   (d) $5\frac{5}{9}\%$

3. Change each decimal to a percentage.
   (a) $0.31 = 0.31 \times 100\%$
       $= \underline{\hspace{2em}}$

   (b) $0.007$

   (c) $1.31$

   (d) $2.075$

4. Convert each percentage to a decimal.
   (a) $29\% = \frac{29}{100}$
       $= \underline{\hspace{2em}}$

   (b) $9\%$

   (c) $129\%$

   (d) $0.9\%$

**5.** Convert each fraction to a decimal and to a percentage.

    **(a)**   $\frac{11}{16}$                                        **(b)**   $4\frac{3}{50}$

**6.**   **(a)**   Express $1\frac{4}{9}$ and 1.45 as percentages.

    **(b)**   Which number, $1\frac{4}{9}$ or 1.45, is smaller?

**7.**   **(a)**   Express $\frac{13}{20}$ as a percentage.

    **(b)**   Express 1.36 as a percentage.

    **(c)**   Work out $\frac{13}{20} + 1.36 - 166\frac{2}{3}\%$ and express the answer as a percentage.

**8.** In a recipe for bolognese sauce, $\frac{1}{3}$ of the total mass of ingredients is meat and 0.36 of the total mass of ingredients is tomatoes. Find the combined total percentage of meat and tomatoes, by mass, in the recipe.

**9.** In a money box, $\frac{3}{8}$ of the coins are £2 coins and 0.28 of the coins are £1 coins. Find the percentage of other coins in the box.

**SCIENCE**
**10.** In a compound, 0.25 of the atoms are carbon, $\frac{2}{3}$ of the atoms are hydrogen and the rest are oxygen. What is the percentage of oxygen atoms in the compound?

**PROBLEM SOLVING**
**11.** In a flat, $\frac{2}{5}$ of the area is the living room and 0.16 of the area is the kitchen. Bedrooms take up 30% of the area. Work out the percentage of the area that other parts of the flat take up.

# 4.2 Simple Percentage Problems

## ⚙ LEVEL 1

1. Express $A$ as a percentage of $B$ in each case.
   (a) $A = £12$, $B = £60$         (b) $A = 35\,\text{km}$, $B = 25\,\text{km}$

2. Express $N$ as a percentage of $M$ in each case.
   (a) $M = 56\,\text{min}$, $N = 49\,\text{min}$      (b) $M = 200\,\text{ml}$, $N = 516\,\text{ml}$

3. Calculate these values.
   (a) 45% of £120         (b) 260% of $95\,\text{m}^2$

£ **FINANCE** 4. Ewan's income in one week is £640. He spends £736 on a new computer. What percentage of his weekly income does he spend on the computer?

5. Diana takes 45 minutes to finish an assignment. Joseph takes 120% of the time taken by Diana to finish the same assignment. How long does Joseph take?

**6.** There are 160 Year 8 students. 108 of them participate in Sports Day. Find the percentage of Year 8 students who

    **(a)** participate in Sports Day,

    **(b)** do not participate in Sports Day.

**7.** Of the 75 fruits on a stall, 27 are oranges and 36 are apples. The rest are pears.

    **(a)** What percentage of the fruits are oranges?

    **(b)** What percentage of the fruits are pears?

    **(c)** Express the number of apples as a percentage of the number of pears.

**£ 8.** The interest rate of a savings scheme is 3% per annum.

FINANCE

    **(a)** Pierre deposits £2400 into the scheme for two years. Find the simple interest he will earn in two years.

    **(b)** Sonia deposits £4500 into the scheme. For how many years should she leave her money there so that her simple interest amounts to £675?

9. A job applicant has to take three tests. Altogether the tests have 400 possible marks. The literacy test has 40% of the marks. The numeracy test has 35% of the marks. The aptitude test has the rest of the marks.

(a) Work out the number of marks for the numeracy test.

(b) Work out the number of marks for the aptitude test.

(c) Express the number of marks for the literacy test as a percentage of the number of marks for the aptitude test.

**PROBLEM SOLVING**

10. There are 350 flowers in a garden. 40% of the flowers are roses. 20% of the roses are pink.

(a) What is the number of pink roses in the garden?

(b) Find the percentage of the flowers which are pink roses.

**£ FINANCE**

11. (a) Eva borrows £3600 from a bank for four years. The interest is calculated by simple interest at 5% per annum. How much interest will she pay to the bank?

(b) William borrows £3000 from another lender for five years. The interest is calculated by simple interest at 6% per annum. How much interest will he pay to the lender?

(c) Express the interest paid by William as a percentage of the interest paid by Eva.

# 4.3 Reverse Percentages

1. Find the unknown quantity in each case.
   (a) 20% of $m$ kg is 14 kg.           (b) 120% of $L$ cm is 78 cm.

2. 30% of Year 8 students cycle to school. There are 48 Year 8 students who cycle to school. Find the total number of Year 8 students.

3. Patrick got 126 votes in a club election. This was 45% of the total number of votes. What was the total number of votes?

4. In a journey from Oxford to Cambridge, a car travels on motorways for 95% of the total distance. The distance travelled on motorways is 128.25 km. Find the total journey distance from Oxford to Cambridge.

**5.** 65% of the staff in a company are female and the rest are male. There are 52 female staff. Find
    **(a)** the total number of staff in the company,

    **(b)** the number of male staff in the company.

**6.** Ann uses 27% of her savings to buy a coat. The price of the coat is £216.
    **(a)** How much were her savings?

    **(b)** After buying the coat, how much of her savings does she have left?

**7.** The area of a living room is $21\,\text{m}^2$. This is 175% of the area of a bedroom.
    **(a)** Find the area of the bedroom.

    **(b)** Express the area of the bedroom as a percentage of the area of the living room.

**8.** A copper rod is 25% shorter than an iron rod. The total length of the two rods is 315 cm. Find the length of the iron rod.

**9.** The number of £5 notes in a till is 30% more than the number of £10 notes. There are six more £5 notes than £10 notes in the till. Find the total value of these banknotes.

**10.** A sum of money is deposited in an investment bond. It earns simple interest at the rate of 5% per annum. The total interest for four years is £460.

(a) Calculate the sum of money deposited at the start.

(b) If the original sum were instead deposited into another bond which offers 6% per annum simple interest, after how many years would the interest be greater than £400?

# 4.4 Percentage Increase and Decrease

## ⚙ LEVEL 1

1. The daily wage of a worker increases from £120 to £138. Find the percentage increase in the wage.

2. The price of a TV decreases from £500 to £430. Find the percentage decrease in the price.

3. The volume of a balloon is initially 650 cm³. The volume is then increased by 18%. Calculate
   (a) the increase in volume,

   (b) the new volume of the balloon.

4. Mr Taylor's electricity bill in January was £120. In February his bill was 10% less. Calculate
   (a) the decrease in the bill,

   (b) the electricity bill in February.

5. The mass of a newborn baby boy is 3.0 kg. His mass increases by 200% in the first year. Find his mass at the end of the first year.

**6.** The floor area of a house is increased by 6% to 265 m$^2$ in a renovation. Find the original floor area.

**7.** After cutting off the top 25% of a tree, the height of the tree becomes 240 cm. Find its original height.

**8.** A rectangle on a designer's computer screen is 80 mm long and 60 mm high. When she drags a corner of the rectangle, its length and height increase by the same percentage. If the length increases to 108 mm, what is the new height?

**9.** The usual price of a dishwasher is £680 and that of a cooker is £960. The prices are reduced by the same percentage in a sale. The reduced price of the dishwasher is £646. Find the reduced price of the cooker.

**£**  **10.** The price of a new car is £28 000. Its value decreases by 20% after one year.

**FINANCE**

   **(a)** Find the car's value after one year.

   **(b)** Its value at the end of the second year is 15% less than its value at the end of the first year. Find its value after two years.

**£**  **11.** The price of a necklace is £450. The jewellery shop increases its price by 20% and then sells it at a

**FINANCE**  discount of 20%.

   **(a)** Calculate the selling price of the necklace.

   **(b)** Express the selling price as a percentage of the original price.

**£**  **12.** **(a)** In a bakery, the price of a fruit cake is £5.00. The price is decreased by 10% in a promotion.

**FINANCE**  What is the new price?

**PROBLEM SOLVING**

   **(b)** After decreasing the price, the number of fruit cakes sold in a week increases by 15% to 1380. What was the original number of cakes sold per week?

   **(c)** Does the total revenue from the sales of the cakes increase or decrease? What is the percentage change?

# Review 1

Answer all the questions.

Section A (Short Questions)

1.  Given the numbers 4, 5, 17, 23, 36, 55, 57, 68, write down the number which is
    (a) a factor of 34,

    (b) a multiple of 11,

    (c) a prime number and is not a factor of 85.

2.  Express 1500 as the product of its prime factors in index notation.

3.  Let $a = 2^2 \times 3 \times 7^3$ and $b = 2 \times 3^4 \times 7^2 \times 11$. Leaving your answers as a product of prime factors in index notation, write down
    (a) the HCF of $a$ and $b$,

    (b) the LCM of $a$ and $b$.

4.  (a) Estimate the value of $3278 + 5630 - 254$ by rounding each number to one significant figure.

    (b) Work out the value of $3278 + 5630 - 254$ and round your answer to three significant figures.

**5.** The photo shows a man walking with his elephant. The man is 1.65 m tall. Estimate the height of the elephant to the nearest 0.1 m. Explain your working.

**6.** A bag contains red, green and blue balls. The ratio of the number of red balls to the number of green balls is 4:3. The ratio of the number of green balls to the number of blue balls is 2:5.

    **(a)** Find the ratio red balls : green balls : blue balls.

    **(b)** If there are 87 balls in the bag, find the number of red balls.

**7.** On a particular day, the exchange rate between the British pound (GBP) and the US dollar (USD) is 1 GBP = 1.35 USD.

    **(a)** The price of a handbag is 120 GBP. Express its price in US dollars.

    **(b)** The price of a watch is 378 USD. Express its price in British pounds.

**8.** Harry takes 1 hour 40 minutes to drive 130 km from Birmingham to Warrington. He then continues for a further 40 minutes at an average speed of 72 km/h from Warrington to Preston. Calculate his average speed in km/h

    **(a)** from Birmingham to Warrington,

**(b)** for the whole journey from Birmingham to Preston, giving your answer to three significant figures.

**£ 9.** A sum of £1800 is deposited in a savings account for three years at the simple interest rate of 4% per
**FINANCE** annum. How much interest does the sum earn over the three years?

**10.** The selling price of a dress in a boutique is £324. The boutique gets 35% profit on its cost. Find the cost of the dress to the boutique.

**Section B (Structured Questions)**

**11. (a)** Express 240 as the product of its prime factors in index notation.

**(b)** Find the HCF of 75 and 240.

**(c)** In a hardware shop, each box of screws contains 240 screws and each pack of hinges contains 75 hinges. Stella wants to buy the same number of screws and hinges. Find the smallest number of boxes of screws that she could buy.

**12.** Seven cans of paint can cover $84\,\text{m}^2$ of wall.

   **(a)** Find the area covered per can of paint.

   **(b)** How many cans should be bought to cover $130\,\text{m}^2$ of wall?

   **(c)** In painting a wall, the paint cost and the labour cost are in the ratio $2:5$. A painting job needs £60 of paint. How much is the total cost of the job?

**13.** **(a)** Dame Kelly Holmes won the 800 m event at the Athens Summer Olympics 2004. Her time for the race was 1 minute 56.38 seconds. Calculate her average speed in this race, giving your answer to the nearest $0.1\,\text{m/s}$.

   **(b)** In Kelly Holmes' international competitions, the ratio of her gold medals to her silver medals was $7:8$. The ratio of her silver medals to her bronze medals was $2:1$. She won four bronze medals. Find the total number of medals that she won.

**14.** Amy and David both have a monthly salary of £2500. Amy's salary increases by 30% after two years. David's salary increases by 20% after one year, then increases by 10% at the end of the second year. After two years, what is

   **(a)** Amy's salary,

   **(b)** David's salary,

**(c)** the ratio of Amy's salary to David's salary, in its simplest form?

**15.** A gym has 800 members. The ratio of gold members to silver members is $2:3$.
**(a)** Find the number of gold members and the number of silver members.

**(b)** The number of gold members increases by 30%.
**(i)** If the total number of members is unchanged, find the percentage decrease in the number of silver members.

**(ii)** If the number of silver members decreases by 15%, find the overall percentage change in the number of gym members.

## 5.1 Use of Letters in Algebra

### ⚙ LEVEL 1

1. Deanne drives from her home to her office, which is 40 km away. What is her distance from the office after driving

   (a) 13 km?

   27 km

   (b) $d$ km?

   $40 - d$ km

2. A prize of £2400 is shared equally among a team of football players. Find the amount each player gets if there are

   (a) 15 players,

   £160

   (b) $m$ players.

   $2400 \div m$    $\dfrac{2400}{m}$

3. Simplify these expressions.

   (a) $a \times 5 \times a$

   $5a^2$

   (b) $3b \times 7c$

   $21bc$

   (c) $5m \div 8n$

   $\dfrac{5m}{8n}$

   (d) $p \div 6 - q \times 11$

   $\dfrac{p}{6} - 11q$

4. Write these statements as algebraic expressions.

   (a) Subtract $6a$ from the product of $3b$ and $c^3$.

   $3bc^3 - 6a$

   (b) Divide the sum of $2x$ and $5y$ by $7z$.

   $\dfrac{2x + 5y}{7z}$

5.  A box of chocolates costs £6. A box of biscuits costs £4. Find the total price of
    **(a)** two boxes of chocolates and five boxes of biscuits,

    32

    **(b)** $m$ boxes of chocolates and $n$ boxes of biscuits.

    $(6 \times m) + (4 \times n)$    $6m + 4n$

6.  A mathematics book is 2 cm thick. A dictionary is 5 cm thick. Find the total height of a stack of
    **(a)** three mathematics books and four dictionaries,

    26    $(2 \times 3 = 6) + (5 \times 4 = 20)$

    **(b)** $p$ mathematics books and $q$ dictionaries.

    $(p \times 2) + (9 \times 5) = p2$    $2p + 5q$

7.  There are 500 grams of butter in a refrigerator. Find the remaining amount of butter if
    **(a)** 40 grams are used for cooking and 130 grams are used for baking,

    **(b)** $c$ grams are used for cooking and $b$ grams are used for baking.

8.  There are 1500 ml of milk in a jug. Find the remaining amount of milk in the jug after
    **(a)** 8 cups of coffee are each topped up with 90 ml of milk from the jug,

    $8 \times 90 = 720ml$    $1500 - 720 = \boxed{780ml}$

    **(b)** $x$ cups of coffee are each topped up with $y$ ml of milk from the jug.

    $x \times y = xy$    $1500 - xy$

9.  A metal bar is 156 cm long. A length of $L$ cm is cut from it. The remaining length is cut into $m$ equal
    pieces. Express the length of each piece in terms of $L$ and $m$.

    New length = $\dfrac{156 - L}{m}$

10. Kylie's age is four years more than three times her daughter's age. Find Kylie's age if her daughter is
    (a) 11 years old, 37

    $11 \times 3 + 4 = 37$

    (b) *n* years old.

    $(n \times 3) + 4$

11. A bag weighs *B* grams. A squash ball weighs 24 grams. A tennis ball weighs 57 grams. Find the total mass of a bag containing
    (a) three squash balls and four tennis balls,

    228

    B2    $24 \times 3 = 72$    $57 \times 4 = 228$    $= 300 + b$

    (b) *s* squash balls and *t* tennis balls.

    24st    $24s + 57t + B$

12. In his triathlon training, Paul swims *s* km.
    (a) His running distance is 10 km more than twice his swimming distance. Express his running distance in terms of *s*.

    $s \times 2 + 10 km$    2s+10    $2s+10$

    (b) His cycling distance is 5 km less than three times his running distance. Express his cycling distance in terms of *s*.

    $3(2s+10)$    $6s + 30 - 5$    $6s + 25$

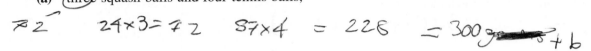

13. In a compound of carbon, hydrogen and oxygen, there is one oxygen atom. The number of hydrogen atoms is two more than twice the number of carbon atoms. Find the total number of atoms in the compound if there are
    (a) three carbon atoms,

    8 (12)    $3 \times 2 = 6 + 2 = 8 \text{ hydrogen} + 1 = 9$

    (b) *n* carbon atoms.

    $2n + 2 = h + 1 + n$

    $2n + 2 + 1 + n$

    (3n+3)

## 5.2 Evaluation of Algebraic Expressions and Formulae

### ⚙ LEVEL 1

**1.** Work out the value of $3n + 7$ when
    **(a)** $n = 5$,
                         **(b)** $n = -8$.

$22$
                                              $-17$

**2.** Find the value of $\dfrac{24}{2p-3}$ when
    **(a)** $p = 0$,
                         **(b)** $p = 3$.

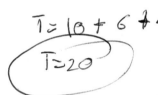
                          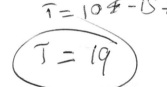

**3.** Given that $T = 10 + 3u - 4v$, find the value of $T$ if
    **(a)** $u = 2$ and $v = -1$,
                **(b)** $u = -5$ and $v = -6$.

$T = 10 + 6 + 4$
               $T = 10 + -15 + 24$

$\boxed{T = 20}$
                 $\boxed{T = 19}$

**4.** Given the formula $V = \overset{9}{\cancel{3}}{}^{S} h$, calculate the value of $V$ when $x = 3$ and $h = 5$.

$V = 845$

**5.** Given the formula $S = 6p - 3q^2$, work out the value of $S$ if $p = 8$ and $q = -2$.

**6.** Find the value of $3a(b - c)$ when
   **(a)** $a = 4$, $b = 7$ and $c = -1$,
   **(b)** $a = -5$, $b = -3$ and $c = 6$.

$3 \times 4 (7 - -1) = 12(8)$
$\boxed{96}$

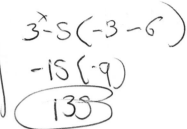

$3 \times -5(-3 - 6)$
$-15(-9)$
$\boxed{135}$

**7.** Work out the value of $p^2 - q^2 + 3r^2$ when
   **(a)** $p = 2$, $q = 3$ and $r = 1$,
   **(b)** $p = -4$, $q = -2$ and $r = 5$.

$4 - 9 + 3 = \boxed{-2}$

$16 - 4 + 75$
$12 + 75$
$\boxed{87}$

**8.** Given that $E = \dfrac{1}{2} m(v^2 - u^2)$, calculate the value of $E$ when
   **(a)** $m = 3$, $u = 5$ and $v = 1$,
   **(b)** $m = 4$, $u = 3$ and $v = 11$.

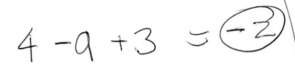

$E \, \frac{1}{2} 3 (1^2 - 5^2) =$

$E \frac{1}{2} 3 (1 - 25) = E = \frac{1}{2} 3 - 75)$

$= \boxed{E = 1.5 - 37.5 = \boxed{-36}}$

$E = \frac{1}{2} 4 (11^2 - 3^2)$
$E = 2(121 - 9)$
$E = 242 - 18$ $\boxed{M = 224}$

**9.** If $T = \dfrac{mn}{p^3 + 1}$, calculate the value of $T$ when
   **(a)** $m = 8$, $n = 35$ and $p = 3$,
   **(b)** $m = -21$, $n = 10$ and $p = -2$.

$T = \dfrac{8 \times 35}{3^3 + 1}$    $T = \dfrac{280}{28}$
$\boxed{T = 10}$

$T = \dfrac{-21 \times 10}{-2^3 + 1} = $    $T = \dfrac{-210}{7}$
$\boxed{T = -30}$

**10.** If $y = kx^{n+1}$, work out the value of $y$ when
   **(a)** $k = 5$, $x = 4$ and $n = 2$,
   **(b)** $k = -7$, $x = 6$ and $n = 0$.

$y = 5 \times 4^{2+1} =$
$y = 20^3$   $\boxed{y = 8,000}$

$k = -7 \times 4 = 6$ and $2 = 0$
$-7 \times 6 = \boxed{-42}$

**11.** The price for *n* tickets for a concert is given by the expression £25*n*.

**FINANCE**

(a) Find the price for four tickets.

£100

(b) What does the number 25 in the expression 25*n* represent?

Price per ticket

 **12.** The power *P* watts of an electrical appliance is given by the formula $P = VI$, where *V* volts is the

**SCIENCE** voltage of the appliance and *I* amperes is the current through the appliance. Find the power of a heater if the voltage is 200 volts and the current is 7 amperes.

$P = 1400$

**13.** The parking space for a car is $12\,m^2$ and the parking space for a motorcycle is $4\,m^2$. A car park has *m* parking spaces for cars and *n* parking spaces for motorcycles.

(a) Express the total parking space for cars and motorcycles in terms of *m* and *n*.

12M +4n

(b) The total area of the car park is $400\,m^2$ and the area not used for parking spaces is $A\,m^2$. Write a formula connecting *m*, *n* and *A*.

12M + 4n + A = 400    a = 400 − 12m + 4n

(c) If *m* = 24 and *n* = 10, find the value of *A*.

288    40

a = 400 − 288 − 40    A = 72

(d) Explain why you would not want *A* to be 0.

because then the cars couldn't park

# 5.3 Algebraic Expressions in the Real World

## ⚙ LEVEL 1

1. The bar model shows the prices of two books, where the price of book A is £2x.

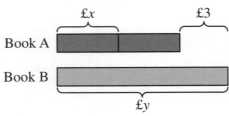

   (a) Express $y$ in terms of $x$.

   *[handwritten:]* $\frac{6}{3}$  $2x + 3 = y$

   (b) If $x = 5$, find the price of book B.

   *[handwritten:]* $\underline{\underline{5}}$ 13

2. The bar model shows two pieces of ribbon cut from a long ribbon.

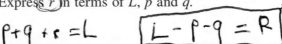

   (a) Express $r$ in terms of $L$, $p$ and $q$.

   *[handwritten:]* $p + q + r = L$  $\boxed{L - p - q = R}$

   (b) The ribbon is 127 cm long. Piece 1 is 48 cm long and piece 2 is 37 cm long. Find the length of the remaining piece.

   *[handwritten:]*
   $\begin{array}{r} 48 \\ +37 \\ \hline 85 \end{array}$   $\begin{array}{r} 127 \\ -85 \\ \hline 42\,cm \end{array}$

3. The bar model shows the capacities of a pot and a bucket.

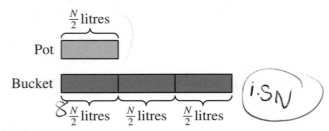

   *[handwritten:]* i.SN

   (a) Express the capacity of the bucket in terms of $N$.

   (b) If $N = 8$, find the capacity of the bucket.

   *[handwritten:]* ⬭12

4. The total mass of an apple and an orange is 450 grams. Let $x$ grams be the mass of the apple.

    **(a)** Express the mass of the orange in terms of $x$.

     $450g - x = 0$

    **(b)** The mass of the apple is 230 grams. Find the mass of the orange.

    $220 g$

5. Amir takes three seconds more to run 200 m than twice the time he takes to run 100 m. Let $T$ seconds be his time taken to run 100 m.

    **(a)** Express his time taken to run 200 m in terms of $T$.

     $2T + 3$

    **(b)** If he takes 12 seconds to run 100 m, how many seconds does he take to run 200 m?

    $27$

6. In a company, the number of female staff is six more than half of the number of male staff. Let $m$ be the number of male staff and $f$ be the number of female staff.

    **(a)** Express $f$ in terms of $m$.

     $f = 6 + 2m$   $f = 0.5m + 6$

    **(b)** If there are 18 male staff, find the number of female staff.

    $15$

7. A tank contains 25 litres of water initially. A tap pours 12 litres of water into the tank every minute. Let $V$ litres be the volume of water in the tank after $t$ minutes.

    **(a)** Express $V$ in terms of $t$.

    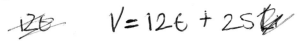 $V = 12t + 25t$

    **(b)** Find the volume of water in the tank after six minutes.

    $97 L$

$x \quad 10+x \quad 20+2x$

**8.** The process of making a frame involves cutting, welding and finishing. The time taken for welding is 10 minutes more than the time for cutting. The time for finishing is twice the time for welding. Let $x$ minutes be the time for cutting.

**(a)** Express the time for welding and the time for finishing in terms of $x$.

$w = y \quad f = z \quad y = 10 + x$

$z = 20 + 2x$

**(b)** Let $T$ minutes be the time required to make the frame. Find a formula connecting $x$ and $T$.

$T = 10 + 4x \qquad T = 30 + 4x$

**(c)** If the time for cutting is 15 minutes, find the time required to make the frame.

$c = 15$
$w = 25$
$f = 50$

90 minutes

**9.** Let $n$ be a date number in the first two weeks of a month.

**(a)** Express, in terms of $n$, the next two date numbers that are on the same day of the week as $n$.

| MON | TUE | WED | THU | FRI | SAT | SUN |
|-----|-----|-----|-----|-----|-----|-----|
|     |     |     | 1   | 2   | 3   | 4   |
| 5   | 6   | 7   | 8   | 9   | 10  | 11  |
| 12  | 13  | 14  | 15  | 16  | 17  | 18  |
| 19  | 20  | 21  | 22  | 23  | 24  | 25  |
| 26  | 27  | 28  | 29  | 30  | 31  |     |

$n + 7$

$n + 14$

**(b)** Let $S$ be the sum of $n$ and the two numbers in **(a)**. Write a formula connecting $n$ and $S$.

$S = n + n + 7 + n + 14$

$S = 3n + 21$

**(c)** Hence find the value of $S$ when $n = 8$.

$S = 45$

# 5.4 Simplification of Linear Expressions

## ⚙ LEVEL 1

**1.** Expand these expressions.

(a) $2(4 + a)$

$8 + 2a$

(b) $5(3b - 2)$

$15b - 10$

(c) $(5c - 6)(4)$

$20c - 24$

(d) $(1 + 7d)(6)$

$6 + 42D$

**2.** Expand these expressions.

(a) $-3(2m + 5)$

$-6m - 15$

(b) $-6(1 - 3n)$

(c) $(4p - 7q)(-5)$

$-20p + 35q$

(d) $(-3r - 8s)(-9)$

**3.** Simplify these expressions.

(a) $2(a + 3) + 3(a + 8)$

$2a + 6 + 3a + 24$

$5a + 30$

(b) $5(2b + 1) + 4(b + 7)$

$10b + 5 + 4b + 28$

$14b + 33$

(c) $(2c - d)(6) + 5(-4c + 3d)$

(d) $(3m - 2n)(7) + 3(2m - n)$

$21m - 14n + \overset{6}{8}m - 3n$

$27m - 17n$

**4.** Simplify these expressions.

(a) $3(p + 5) - 2(4p + 6)$

$3p + 15 - \overset{8}{6}p + 12$

$\boxed{-5p + 3}$

(b) $5(2q - 1) - 4(q - 3)$

(c) $(3r - s)(-7) - 2(5r - 9s)$

$-21r + 7s - 10r + 18s$

$\cancel{3r} - 31r + 25s$

(d) $(-2x + y)(6) - 8(-3x + 4y)$

**5.** Expand these expressions.

(a) $2(3a + 4b + 1)$

$6a + 8b + 2$

(b) $5(2c - 3d + 6)$

(c) $4(3g - 4h - 7k)$

$12g - 16h - 28k$

(d) $(-2m - 5n + 3p)(7)$

**6.** Expand these expressions.

(a) $-3(2q + 3r + 4)$

(b) $-4(2s - 5t - 1)$

(c) $-5(u - 2v + 3w)$

(d) $(-2x - 8y - 9z)(-2)$

**7.** Expand these expressions.

(a) $a(3x + 2y)$

$3xa + 2ya$

(b) $-2b(5p - q)$

(c) $c(4m - 5n)$

$4mc - 5nc$

(d) $(4r - 5s)(-d)$

**8.** Simplify these expressions.

(a) $3(2a + 3b + 1) + 4(3a - 4b - 5)$

$6a + 9b + 3 + 12a - 16b - 20$         $18a\!\!\!\!/ - 7b - 17$

(b) $(x - 5y)(-3) - (3x - 5y + z)(7)$

 **9.** The usual price of a shirt is £p. There is a discount of £10 on each shirt.

(a) Express the total sale price of n shirts in terms of n and p in expanded form, i.e. without using brackets.

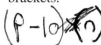 

$(p-10)(n)$  $(p-10)(n)$  $np - 10n$

(b) If the usual price of a shirt is £23, find the total sale price of five shirts.

£115  $p = 23$  $n = 5$

**10.** The width of a chair is $(2x + 7)$ cm. Seven chairs can be placed along a wall, leaving a gap of 30 cm at one end. Let $L$ cm be the length of the wall.

(a) Express $L$ in terms of $x$.

  $L = (2x + 7) \times (7) + 30$

$L = 14x + 49 + 30$  ↑79

(b) If $x = 25$, find the length of the wall.

$L = 350 + 79$  $L = 429$

**11.** The frame for a window consists of six rectangles of width $(3x + y)$ cm and height $(x + 2y)$ cm as shown.

(a) Express the total length of the material used to make the frame in terms of $x$ and $y$ in expanded form.

$6(3x + y)$  $18x + 6y$

$8(x + 2y)$

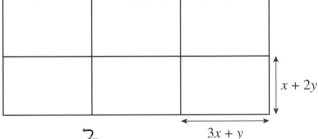

$x + 2y$

$3x + y$

$8x + 16y$  $26x + 24y$  2

(b) If $x = 8$ and $y = 6$, find the total length of the material used to make the frame.

$208 + 132$  340

# 5.5 Proof

## ⚙ LEVEL 1

1. Determine whether or not each of these is a statement. If it is a statement, state whether it is a true statement or a false statement.
   (a) $1 \times 2 \times 3 \times 4 = 24$




   (b) $1 \times 2 \times 3 \times 4$




   (c) Volume of a cube = edge length × edge length




   (d) Odd number + odd number = even number




2. Prove the statement 'If $n$ is an even number, then $n - 1$ is an odd number.'




3. Prove the statement 'If $a$ is an odd number and $b$ is an even number, then $a - b$ is an odd number.'




4. Prove the statement 'If $m$ is a multiple of 6, then $m$ is a multiple of 3.'

**5.** If $n$ is a multiple of 8, show that $\dfrac{n}{4}$ is an integer.

**6.** If $m$ is an even number, show that $m^2$ is a multiple of 4.

**7.** Given that $p$ is a multiple of 7 and $q$ is a multiple of 3, show that the statement
    **(a)** '$pq$ is a multiple of 21' is true,

    **(b)** '$p - q$ is a multiple of 4' is false.

**8.** Jenny found that $1^2 = 1$, $9^2 = 81$ and $11^2 = 121$. The last digit of all these square numbers is 1. She claims that the last digit of the square of an odd number is 1.
    **(a)** Has Jenny correctly proved her claim? Explain your answer.

    **(b)** Show that Jenny's claim is false.

9. Harry worked out that $11 + 12 + 13 = 36$ and $17 + 18 + 19 = 54$. He claimed that 'the sum of three consecutive integers must be even'. Show that his claim is false.

10. If $n$ is an integer, show that
    (a) $6n + 3$ is a multiple of 3,

    (b) $6n + 4$ is an even number,

    (c) $6n + 5$ is an odd number.

11. If $m$ and $n$ are multiples of 5, show that the statement
    (a) '$m + n$ is a multiple of 10' is false,

    (b) '$mn$ is a multiple of 25' is true.

12. Lisa proposes that 'if $p$ is a prime number, then $p + 1$ must not be a prime number.' Show that her proposal is not true.

# 6 Equations and Inequalities in One Variable

When a solution involves a fraction, express it in its lowest terms. An improper fraction should be written as a mixed number.

## 6.1 Simple Linear Equations in One Variable

### ⚙ LEVEL 1

1. Solve these equations.
   (a) $x + 7 = 11$

   (b) $x - 12 = -15$

   (c) $\dfrac{x}{3} = -6$

   (d) $4x = 20$

2. Find the value of the unknown in these equations.
   (a) $a + 1.8 = 3.5$

   (b) $b - 4.7 = -6.9$

   (c) $\dfrac{c}{5} = 3.4$

   (d) $7d = -8.4$

3. Find the value of $y$ in these equations.
   (a) $y + \dfrac{1}{2} = \dfrac{3}{8}$

   (b) $y - \dfrac{3}{5} = 1$

   (c) $\dfrac{y}{12} = -\dfrac{3}{4}$

   (d) $-\dfrac{y}{5} = \dfrac{8}{15}$

4. Solve these equations.
   (a) $2t + 3 = -10$

   (b) $-3 - 5z + 4 = 0$

 **LEVEL 2**

**5.** Find the value of $x$ satisfying each equation.

(a) $4x = x + 7$

(b) $3x - 1 = 2x + 5$

(c) $9 - x = 7x - 1$

(d) $-2x + 3 = 1 - 6x$

**6.** Find the value of the unknown in these equations.

(a) $3p = 5p - 2.8$

(b) $7q - 2.3 = 4q + 1.6$

(c) $6r + \dfrac{4}{3} = 4r$

(d) $-\dfrac{3}{8} + 2s = \dfrac{1}{4} - 3s$

**7.** Solve these equations.

(a) $3t + 6t - 7 = 5t + 1$

(b) $9 - 7x = 1 + 2x - 8x$

(c) $9.2 - 5y + 3.4 = 1.4 + 3y$

(d) $5z - \dfrac{1}{2} - 6z = \dfrac{7}{8} - 3z$

8. Water is dripping from a tap into a basin. The volume of water, $V\,\text{cm}^3$, in the basin at time $t$ minutes is given by the formula $V = 250 + 60t$.

   **(a)** Find the volume of water after four minutes.

   **(b)** After how many minutes will the volume of water be $670\,\text{cm}^3$?

**SCIENCE**

9. After applying the brake, the speed, $v$ m/s, of a car after $t$ seconds is given by the formula $v = 20 - 3t$.

   **(a)** What is the speed of the car after two seconds?

   **(b)** After how many seconds will the car stop?

**PROBLEM SOLVING**

10. A rectangular field is $n$ metres by 3 metres. It is surrounded by a row of square paving slabs of side 1 metre.

    **(a)** Express the number of paving slabs in terms of $n$.

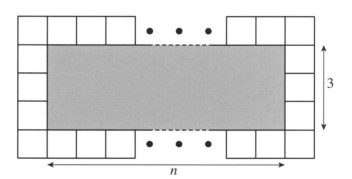

    **(b)** If there are 38 paving slabs, find the value of $n$.

# 6.2 Equations Involving Brackets

 LEVEL 1

1.  Solve these equations.

    **(a)** $5(8 - t) = 11$                  **(b)** $2(3x + 1) = -13$

    **(c)** $3(7 - 2p) = -4$            **(d)** $31 = -3(q - 6)$

2.  Solve these equations.

    **(a)** $5x = 3(x - 2.4)$            **(b)** $-3y = 4(y + 6.3)$

    **(c)** $2(3m) = 3\left(m + \dfrac{4}{9}\right)$       **(d)** $-4\left(2x - \dfrac{1}{3}\right) = \dfrac{5}{6}$

3.  Find the value of $x$ in each equation.

    **(a)** $5(x - 7) = 3(1 - 2x)$        **(b)** $4(2x + 1) = 3(6x - 5)$

    **(c)** $3(4x - 7) - 5(2x - 1) = 0$     **(d)** $7(1 - 2x) + 2(3x + 5) = 0$

4. Solve these equations.

   (a) $3(u - 9) + 5(u - 6) = 7$

   (b) $32 = 5(4 - y) + 3(y + 2)$

   (c) $4(2x - 3) - 5 = 7(x - 4)$

   (d) $6(5x - 2) = 2(1 - x) + 18$

5. Solve these equations.

   (a) $8n - 3(n + 5) = 2(n - 1)$

   (b) $3(1 - 5p) + 7p = 9(4 - p)$

   (c) $5 - 2(q + 3.6) = 3(2q - 1.8)$

   (d) $3(2r - 1) - 7(r + 2) = 5(5 - 3r)$

6. A boy runs a 400 m race. His distance, $D$ m, from the finishing line at time $t$ seconds is given by the formula $D = 8(50 - t)$.
   (a) Find his distance from the finishing line at $t = 10$.

   (b) After how many seconds will he complete
      (i) the race?

      (ii) the first 300 m of the race?

7. The perimeter $P$ cm of the hexagon in the diagram is given by $P = 2(2a + b)$.
   (a) Find the perimeter when $a = 7$ and $b = 10$.

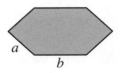

   (b) If $b = 9$ and $P = 46$, find the value of $a$.

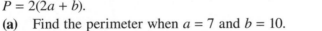

8. Find two possible values of the constant $k$ in the equation $3(2x - 1) = k$ such that the solution for $x$ in the equation is an integer.

# 6.3 Forming Linear Equations to Solve Problems

**1.** Lucy is four times as old as her son, Jack.
Let Jack's age be $x$ years.
   **(a)** Express Lucy's age in terms of $x$.

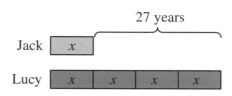

   **(b)** Lucy is 27 years older than Jack. Find Jack's age.

**2.** The volume of juice in a bottle is 175 ml more than the volume of coffee in a cup. Let $x$ ml be the volume of coffee.
   **(a)** Express the volume of juice in terms of $x$.

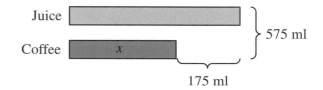

   **(b)** The total volume of juice and coffee is 575 ml.
   Find the volume of coffee.

**3.** There are three consecutive odd integers.
The smallest odd integer is $n$.
   **(a)** Express the middle and the largest odd integers in terms of $n$.

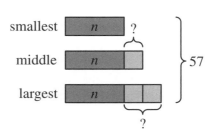

   **(b)** The sum of these three integers is 57.
   Find the three integers.

4.  Polly is three times as old as her daughter, Ava. Six years ago, Polly was four times as old as Ava. Find Ava's age now.

5.  A shop has a total of 20 bicycles and tricycles. The total number of wheels these bicycles and tricycles have is 47. How many tricycles are there?

6.  The price of a watch is £15 more than twice the price of a pen. The total price of the watch and the pen is £111. Find the price of the pen.

7.  In the Rio 2016 Summer Olympics, Great Britain won a total of 67 medals. Of these medals, 27 were gold. The number of silver medals was six more than the number of bronze medals. Find the number of silver medals won.

**8.** In a theme park, the price of a child ticket is £7 less than the price of an adult ticket. The total price for three adult tickets and five child tickets is £93. What is the price of an adult ticket?

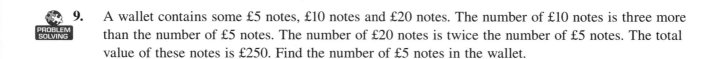

**9.** A wallet contains some £5 notes, £10 notes and £20 notes. The number of £10 notes is three more than the number of £5 notes. The number of £20 notes is twice the number of £5 notes. The total value of these notes is £250. Find the number of £5 notes in the wallet.

**10.** A player scores 39 points in a basketball match. His number of 2-point shots is two less than three times his number of 1-point shots. His number of 3-point shots is one more than his number of 1-point shots. Find his total number of scoring shots.

# 6.4 Solving Simple Inequalities

## ⚙ LEVEL 1

1. Form an inequality to represent a relationship involving the given variable in each statement.
   (a) The body temperature, $T$ °C, is more than 37 °C.

   (b) The volume, $V$ ml, of juice in a box is not less than 375 ml.

   (c) The time taken, $t$ seconds, to run 100 m is less than 11 seconds.

   (d) The speed, $x$ km/h, of a car is not more than 100 km/h.

2. Represent the solutions of each of these inequalities on a number line.
   (a) $x < 2$                                          (b) $x > -1$

   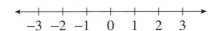                                 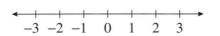

   (c) $x \le \dfrac{1}{2}$                              (d) $x \ge -2\dfrac{3}{4}$

   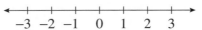                                 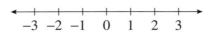

3. Determine whether the given value of $x$ is a solution of the given inequality.
   (a) $x < 5$                                          (b) $x > -3$
       $x = 2$ is/is not a solution.                        $x = -4$ is/is not a solution.

   (c) $x \le -7$                                       (d) $x \ge 8$
       $x = -6$ is/is not a solution.                       $x = 8$ is/is not a solution.

4. If $t > -6$, determine whether or not each of these inequalities is true.
   (a) $t + 5 > -1$                                     (b) $t - 4 > -10$

   (c) $-4t > 24$                                       (d) $\dfrac{t}{3} > -2$

**5.** Fill in each box with an inequality sign.

    **(a)** If $a > b$, then $2 + a$ ☐ $2 + b$.

    **(b)** If $m < n$, then $m - 5$ ☐ $n - 5$.

    **(c)** If $p \leq q$, then $-3p$ ☐ $-3q$.

    **(d)** If $x \geq y$, then $\frac{x}{6}$ ☐ $\frac{y}{6}$.

**6.** Given that $m \geq n$, fill in each box with an inequality sign.

    **(a)** $-3m$ ☐ $-3n$

    **(b)** $10 - 3m$ ☐ $10 - 3n$

    **(c)** $\dfrac{10 - 3m}{17}$ ☐ $\dfrac{10 - 3n}{17}$

**7.** Given that $c > d$, fill in each box with an inequality sign.

    **(a)** $11 + c$ ☐ $11 + d$

    **(b)** $\dfrac{11 + c}{-3}$ ☐ $\dfrac{11 + d}{-3}$

**8.** Given that $h < k$, fill in each box with an inequality sign.

    **(a)** $4h$ ☐ $4k$

    **(b)** $4h + 9$ ☐ $4k + 9$

    **(c)** $11 - 4h$ ☐ $11 - 4k$

**9.** Given that $5x \leq 5y$, fill in each box with an inequality sign.

    **(a)** $x$ ☐ $y$

    **(b)** $x + 6$ ☐ $y + 6$

    **(c)** $20 - \dfrac{x}{3}$ ☐ $20 - \dfrac{y}{3}$

10. The volume of shower gel in a bottle is $x$ ml. It is given that $x > 300$.
    (a) From the given inequality, what can you say about the total volume of shower gel in five of these bottles?

    (b) A new bottle is produced which contains 80 ml of shower gel more than the original bottle. From the given inequality, what can you say about the volume of shower gel in the new bottle?

11. In a shop, the price of every T-shirt is less than £20. Let the price of a T-shirt be £$y$.
    (a) Express the price of one T-shirt as an inequality in terms of $y$.

    (b) A T-shirt is sold at a discount of £3. From the inequality in (a), what can you say about its sale price?

    (c) Another T-shirt is sold at a discount of 50%. From the inequality in (a), what can you say about its sale price?

12. There are five identical balls in a box. The mass of each ball is $m$ grams. The mass of the box is 100 grams. The total mass of the box and the balls is less than 450 grams.
    (a) Express the total mass of the box and the five balls as an inequality in terms of $m$.

    (b) From the inequality in (a), what can you say about the total mass of the balls?

    (c) From the inequality in (b), what can you say about the mass of one ball?

# 7 Coordinates and Linear Functions

## 7.1 Cartesian Coordinate System

⚙ **LEVEL 1**

**1.** **(a)** Write down the coordinates of the points *A* to *H* shown in the diagram.

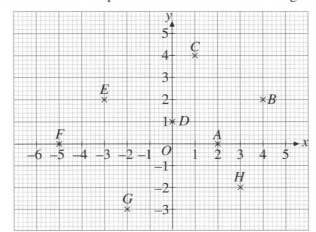

A: _____    B: _____    C: _____    D: _____

E: _____    F: _____    G: _____    H: _____

**(b)** Which point is in the third quadrant?    _____

**(c)** Which points are on the *x*-axis?    _____

**2.** The coordinates of eight points are
$K(3, 2)$, $L(5, 4)$, $M(0, -2)$, $N(-5, 3)$, $P(-2, -3)$, $Q(4, -3)$, $R(-2, 0)$ and $S(-3, -1)$.

**(a)** Plot these points on the coordinate plane.

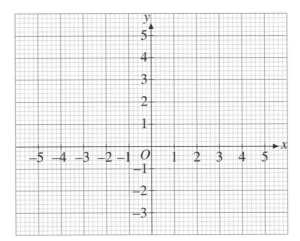

**(b)** Write down the *x*-coordinates of the points *K*, *M* and *R*.

K: _____    M: _____    R: _____

**3.** **(a)** Plot the points $A(-4, 3)$, $B(-1, 1)$ and $C(2, -1)$ on the Cartesian plane.

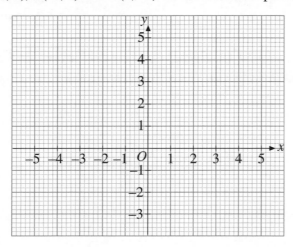

**(b)** Which points are in the second quadrant?  _____

**(c)** Draw the line segments $AB$ and $BC$ on the plane.

**(d)** How are the line segments $AB$ and $BC$ related to each other? Write down two geometrical facts about them.

**4.** **(a)** Plot the points $P(0, 4)$, $Q(-3, 0)$ and $R(0, -2)$ on the Cartesian plane.

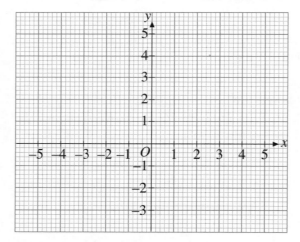

**(b)** Which points are on the $y$-axis?  _____

**(c)** What is the value of the $x$-coordinate of a point on the $y$-axis?  _____

**(d)** Find the area of $\triangle PQR$.

**5.** **(a)** Plot the points $A(6, 4)$, $B(8, 8)$, $C(-2, 6)$, $D(-4, 2)$ and $E(-8, -6)$ on the Cartesian plane and join them successively with line segments. Join $E$ and $A$.

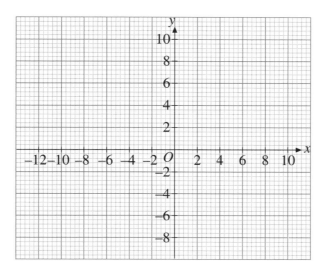

**(b)** What shape do you get? _____

**6.** The diagram shows a map with central London at the origin on a Cartesian plane.

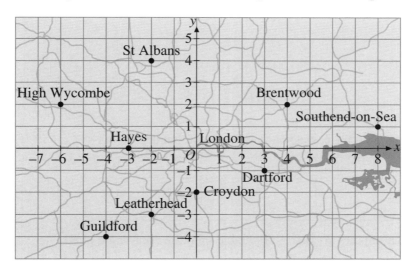

**(a)** Write down the coordinates of these places.
   **(i)** Croydon _____  **(ii)** Brentwood _____

   **(iii)** Guildford _____  **(iv)** High Wycombe _____

**(b)** Name the places located at these coordinates.
   **(i)** (8, 1) _____  **(ii)** (-2, 4) _____

   **(iii)** (-2, -3) _____  **(iv)** (3, -1) _____

**(c)** What is the distance, in units, between Hayes and central London? _____

# 7.2 Idea of a Function

## ⚙ LEVEL 1

1. Express $y$ as a function of $x$ in the form of an equation for each statement.

   **(a)** $y$ is three more than $x$.

   **(b)** $y$ is four times $x$.

   **(c)** $y$ is one-third of $x$.

   **(d)** $y$ is seven less than twice $x$.

2. Find the value of the output $y$ when the input is $x = 4$ for each function machine.

   **(a)**

   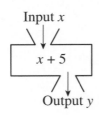

   **(b)**

   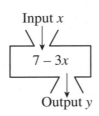

3. A function $y$ of $x$ is given by $y = \dfrac{1}{2}x + 3$.

   **(a)** Complete the table for corresponding values of $x$ and $y$.

   | $x$ | $-4$ | $-2$ | $0$ | $2$ | $4$ |
   |---|---|---|---|---|---|
   | $y$ | | | | | |

   **(b)** Plot the ordered pairs $(x, y)$ from the table onto the coordinate plane.

   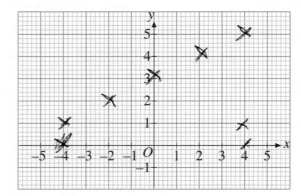

**4.** (−2, 3), (−1, 2), (0, 1) and (3, −2) are four ordered pairs of a function $y$ of $x$.

    **(a)** Which one, $y = x + 3$ or $y = 1 − x$, is the function? Explain your answer.

    **(b)** Find the value of $y$ when $x = 5$.

**5.** Here is a table of values for the function $y = −1 + 2x$.

| $x$ | −2 | −1 | 2 | 3 |
|---|---|---|---|---|
| $y$ | −5 | $p$ | $q$ | 5 |

    **(a)** Work out the values of $p$ and $q$.

    **(b)** Plot the ordered pairs $(x, y)$ of the table on the coordinate plane.

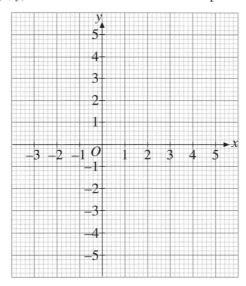

    **(c)** What can you say about the points plotted?

**6.** Let £*y* be the total value of *x* 50p coins.

**(a)** Complete the table of values for *x* and *y*.

| *x* | 2 | 4 | 6 | 8 | 10 |
|---|---|---|---|---|---|
| *y* | | | | | |

**(b)** Using a scale of 1 cm to 1 unit on both axes, plot the ordered pairs (*x*, *y*) from the table onto a coordinate plane.

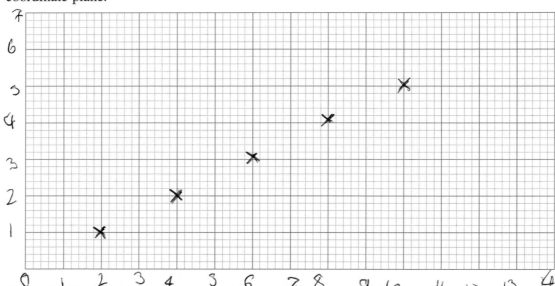

**(c)** Write down an equation connecting *x* and *y*.

7. A cable is 6 metres long. Let $y$ metres be the remaining length of the cable after $x$ metres is cut from it.

   (a) Complete the table of values for $x$ and $y$.

   | $x$ | 1 | 2 | 3 | 4 | 5 |
   |-----|---|---|---|---|---|
   | $y$ |   |   |   |   |   |

   (b) Using a scale of 1 cm to 1 unit on both axes, plot the ordered pairs $(x, y)$ from the table onto a coordinate plane.

   (c) Write down an equation connecting $x$ and $y$.

# 7.3　Linear Functions and their Graphs

⚙ **LEVEL 1**

**1.** **(a)** Complete this table of values.

| $x$ | −4 | −2 | 0 | 2 | 4 |
|---|---|---|---|---|---|
| $y = 5 - x$ | | | | | |

**(b)** Draw the graph of $y = 5 - x$ for values of $x$ from −4 to 4 on the Cartesian plane.

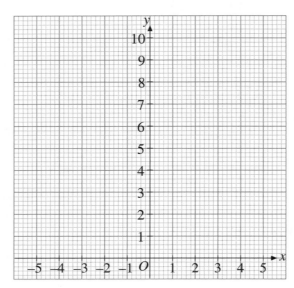

**(c)** Does the point $A(1, 4)$ lie on the graph?

**2.** **(a)** Complete these tables of values.

| $x$ | −4 | −2 | 0 | 2 | 4 |
|---|---|---|---|---|---|
| $y = -\dfrac{1}{2}x + 1$ | | | | | |

| $x$ | −3 | 1 | 3 |
|---|---|---|---|
| $y = 1$ | | | |

**(b)** Draw the graphs of $y = -\dfrac{1}{2}x + 1$ and $y = 1$ for values of $x$ from −4 to 4 on the Cartesian plane.

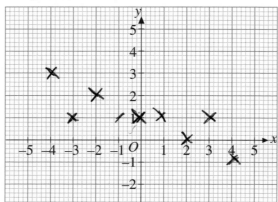

**(c)** At which point do the two graphs meet?　＿＿＿＿＿＿＿＿＿＿

**3.** **(a)** Draw the graphs of these equations on the same diagram for values of $x$ from $-6$ to $6$.

    **(i)**    $y = \dfrac{1}{3}x$                          **(ii)**   $y = \dfrac{1}{3}x + 3$

    **(iii)** $y = \dfrac{1}{3}x + 1$                    **(iv)** $y = \dfrac{1}{3}x - 2$

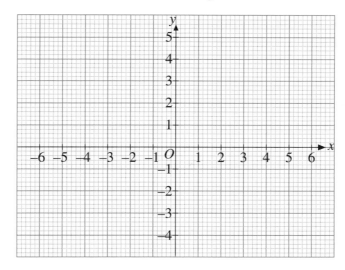

    **(b)** What do you observe about the graphs in **(a)**?

**4.** **(a)** Draw the graph of $y = 10 - 4x$ for $x = -2$ to $x = 4$ using a scale of $1\,\text{cm}$ to $1$ unit on the $x$-axis and $1\,\text{cm}$ to $5$ units on the $y$-axis.

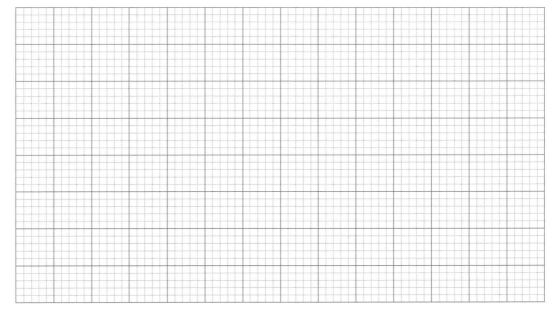

    **(b)** The points $P(0, p)$ and $Q(q, 2)$ lie on the graph. Use the graph to find the values of $p$ and $q$.

5. When an athlete runs a race, her distance $d$ metres from the finishing line after $t$ seconds is given by the equation $d = 400 - 8t$.
   (a) Using a scale of 1 cm to 5 units on the $t$-axis and 1 cm to 100 units on the $d$-axis, draw the graph of $d = 400 - 8t$ for $0 \leq t \leq 50$.

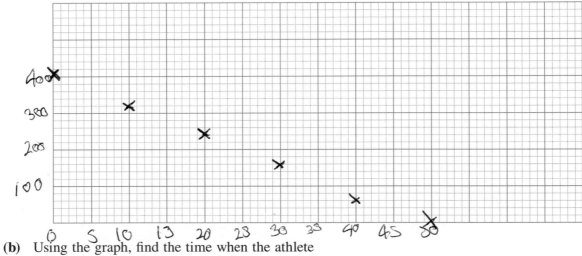

   (b) Using the graph, find the time when the athlete
       (i) is 240 m from the finishing line,

       (ii) completes the race.

   (c) What is the distance of the race?

6. The conversion of $x\,°C$ to $y\,°F$ is given by the equation $y = \dfrac{9}{5}x + 32$.
   (a) Using a scale of 1 cm to 10 units on the $x$-axis and 1 cm to 50 units on the $y$-axis, draw the graph of $y = \dfrac{9}{5}x + 32$ for $0 \leq x \leq 100$.

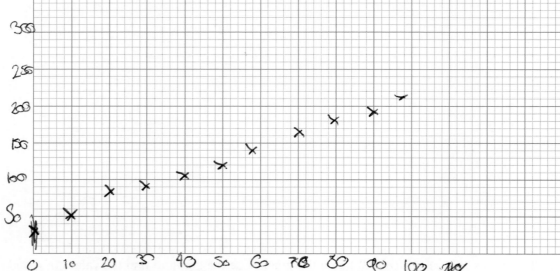

   (b) Using the graph, convert 100 °F to the nearest degree Celsius.

# 7.4  Gradients of Linear Graphs

## ⚙ LEVEL 1

1. Find the gradients of the lines $L_1$, $L_2$ and $L_3$ in the diagram.

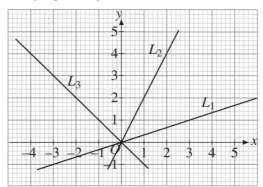

Gradient of $L_1$ = _____     Gradient of $L_2$ = _____     Gradient of $L_3$ = _____

2. Find the gradients of the sides of $\triangle PQR$ in the diagram.

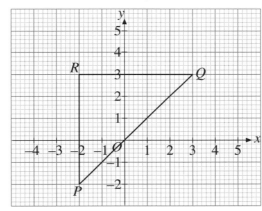

Gradient of side $PQ$ = _____

Gradient of side $QR$ = _____

Gradient of side $PR$ = _____

3. State the gradient and $y$-intercept of each line.
   (a) $y = 3x - 4$

   Gradient = _____     $y$-intercept = _____

   (b) $y = -\dfrac{2}{5}x + 1$

   Gradient = _____     $y$-intercept = _____

4.  Draw a line through each given pair of points on the diagram and find its gradient.

    **(a)**  O(0, 0), A(5, 2)                    **(b)**  B(–3, 1), C(1, –3)

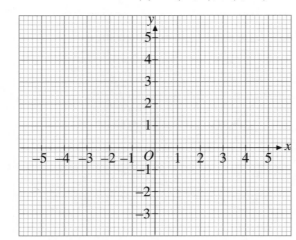

$\dfrac{-2}{-2}$

$\dfrac{5}{2}$

Gradient of OA = $2\,5$ _____

Gradient of BC = _____

5.  **(a)**  Draw the quadrilateral EFGH whose vertices are E(–3, 0), F(2, –1), G(4, 2) and H(–1, 3).

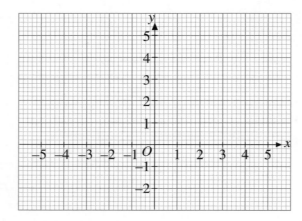

   **(b)**  Find the gradient of each side of EFGH.

   Gradient of EF = _____            Gradient of FG = _____
   Gradient of GH = _____            Gradient of EH = _____

   **(c)**  Which pairs of sides have equal gradients?

   **(d)**  What type of quadrilateral is EFGH?

6. A solution is dripping from a burette into a beaker. The volume, $V$ cm$^3$, of the solution in the beaker at time $t$ seconds is given by the function $V = 5 + 2t$.

   (a) Using a scale of 1 cm to 1 unit on the $t$-axis and 1 cm to 5 units on the $V$-axis, draw the graph of $V = 5 + 2t$ for $0 \leq t \leq 10$.

   (b) State the gradient of the graph and interpret its meaning in this function.

   (c) Interpret the meaning of the constant term 5 in this function.

**7.** The balance, £y, on a travel card after $n$ days is given by the function $y = 40 - 5n$.

    **(a)** Using a scale of 1 cm to 1 unit on the $n$-axis and 1 cm to 10 units on the $y$-axis, draw the graph of $y = 40 - 5n$ for $0 \leq n \leq 8$.

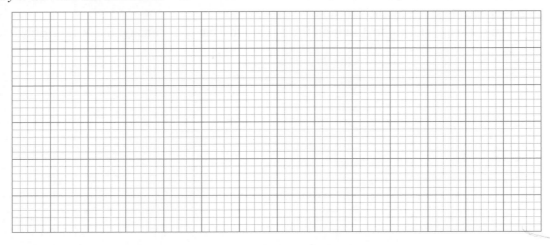

    **(b)** State the gradient of the graph and interpret its meaning in this function.

    **(c)** State the $y$-intercept of the graph and interpret its meaning in this function.

# 8 Number Patterns

## 8.1 Number Patterns and Sequences

### ⚙ LEVEL 1

1. Write down the term-to-term rule and the next two terms of each sequence.
   (a) 2, 5, 8, 11, ...
   14  17
   (b) 23, 18, 13, 8, ... 3  − 2

2. Write down the term-to-term rule and the next two terms of each sequence.
   (a) 3, 12, 48, 192, ... 768, 3072
   (b) 384, 192, 96, 48, ... 24  12

3. Write down the next two terms of each sequence.
   (a) 4, 5, 7, 10, ... 14  19
   (b) $\frac{2}{5}, \frac{4}{7}, \frac{6}{9}, \frac{8}{11}, ...$ $\frac{10}{13}$  $\frac{12}{15}$

4. The first term of a sequence is 23. The term-to-term rule is 'subtract 7'. Work out the 4th term.
   2

5. The first term of a sequence is 72. The term-to-term rule is 'multiply by $-\frac{1}{2}$'. Work out the 4th term.
   −9

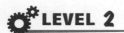

6. Find the 7th term of each sequence.
   (a) 3, 8, 13, 18, ... $\boxed{33}$

   (b) 29, 23, 17, 11, ... $5 \quad -1 \quad \boxed{-7}$

   (c) 6, –12, 24, –48, ... $384$

   (d) 3125, –1250, 500, –200, ... $\boxed{12 \cdot 8}$
   $\underset{83}{\smile} \underset{700}{\smile}$

7. After the first term of a sequence, each term is eight more than the previous term. The second term of the sequence is 17. Find
   (a) the first term,

   (b) the third term,

   (c) the fourth term.

8. A sequence is formed by $4 \times 1^3, 4 \times 2^3, 4 \times 3^3, 4 \times 4^3, \ldots$ .
   (a) Find the values of the first two terms of the sequence.

   (b) Find the value of the 6th term of the sequence.

9. A sequence is formed by $1 \times 3, 2 \times 4, 3 \times 5, 4 \times 6, \ldots$ .
   (a) Find the values of the 3rd term and the 4th term of the sequence.

   (b) Find the value of the 9th term of the sequence.

**10.** The values of an investment in year 1, year 2, year 3 and year 4 are £5000, £7500, £11 250 and £16 875 respectively.

    **(a)** Find the term-to-term rule for these values of the investment.

    **(b)** If the value of the investment continues to grow in this manner, what will be its value in year 6?

**11.** The diagram shows some tile patterns. Each side of a tile is 30 cm.

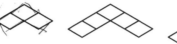 

Position number:      $n = 1$      $n = 2$      $n = 3$

    **(a)** Draw the tile pattern for $n = 4$.

    **(b)** Let $T_n$ be the number of tiles in the $n$th position. Find $T_n$ for $n = 1$ to 5.

    **(c)** If $P_n$ is the perimeter, in centimetres, of the $n$th pattern, find $P_n$ for $n = 1$ to 5.

# 8.2 General Term of a Sequence

1. Find the first three terms of each sequence from the given general term $T_n$.

    (a) $T_n = 2n - 5$

    (b) $T_n = 21 - 3n$

    (c) $T_n = n^2 + 1$

    (d) $T_n = \dfrac{n}{n+3}$

2. The general term of a sequence is $T_n = 768 \times \left(\dfrac{1}{2}\right)^n$. Find the 6th term.

3. Given the arithmetic sequence $x$, 13, 19, 25, 31, ..., find

    (a) the value of $x$,

    (b) the 7th term.

4. Given the geometric sequence $y$, 12, 36, 108, 324, ..., find

    (a) the value of $y$,

    (b) the 6th term.

**5.** **(a)** Express the $n$th term of the sequence 41, 34, 27, 20, … in terms of $n$.

**(b)** Hence find the 12th term of the sequence.

**6.** **(a)** The $n$th term of a sequence is given by $n(n + 4)$. Find the values of the first four terms of the sequence.

**(b)** Hence, express the $n$th term of the sequence 4, 11, 20, 31, … in terms of $n$.

**7.** **(a)** The table shows the number patterns for $p$, $q$ and $r$. Complete Row 5 and Row 6.

|  | $p$ | $q$ | $r$ |
|---|---|---|---|
| Row 1 | 2 $1 \times 2$ | 1 | 1 |
| Row 2 | 6 $2 \times 3$ | 2 | 4 |
| Row 3 | 12 $3 \times 4$ | 3 | 9 |
| Row 4 | 20 $4 \times 5$ | 4 | 16 |
| Row 5 | 3. $5 \times 6$ | 5 | 25 |
| Row 6 | 4.6 $\times 7$ | 6 | 36 |

**(b)** Express $p$, $q$ and $r$ in terms of $n$ in the $n$th row.

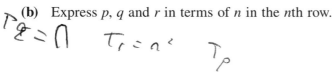

$T_q = n \qquad T_r = n^2 \qquad T_p$

**(c)** Express $r$ in terms of $p$ and $q$.

$r = p - q$

8. The diagram shows a sequence of patterns formed by square tiles. Let $T_n$ be the number of tiles in the position number $n$.

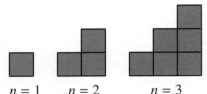

Position number:  $n = 1$   $n = 2$   $n = 3$

(a) Write down the values of the terms $T_4$ and $T_5$.

(b) The $n$th term of the sequence is given by the formula $T_n = \frac{1}{2}n(n+1)$. Verify that the formula is true when $n = 6$.

(c) Use the formula to find the value of $T_{50}$.

(d) Hence find the sum $3 + 6 + 9 + 12 + \ldots + 150$.

9. The diagram shows some stacks of identical cups. The heights when one, three, five and seven cups are stacked up are 15 cm, 21 cm, 27 cm and 33 cm respectively.

(a) Find the height when
   (i) two cups are stacked up,

   (ii) four cups are stacked up.

(b) Let $T_n$ be the height of the stack of $n$ cups. Express $T_n$ in terms of $n$.

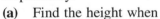

$3n + 12$

(c) If a stack is 75 cm high, how many cups are in the stack?

21

# Review 2

Answer all the questions.

## Section A (Short Questions)

1.  (a) Circle the expression which is equal to $a + 2b$.

    $$2a + b \qquad 2b + a \qquad 2ab \qquad 2(a + b)$$

    (b) Circle the expression which is equal to $3 \times p$.

    $$p \times p \times p \qquad 3p \qquad p^3 \qquad 3^p$$

    (c) Circle the expression which is equal to $m \times m \times m \times m$.

    $$4m \qquad 3m \times m^3 \qquad m^3 \qquad m^2 \times m^2$$

**£ 2.** The price of a shirt is £30. The price of a tie is £13.

FINANCE

(a) Express the price of $m$ shirts and $n$ ties in terms of $m$ and $n$.

(b) Hence find the price of three shirts and two ties.

3.  (a) Simplify $3(2p + q) - 5(p - 4q)$.

    (b) Hence find the value of $3(2p + q) - 5(p - 4q)$ when $p = 7$ and $q = -6$.

4.  Given the formula $S = (n - 2) \times 180$, find
    (a) the value of $S$ when $n = 7$,

    (b) the value of $n$ when $S = 540$.

5. **(a)** Solve the equation $8(x - 1) = 5(2x + 3)$.

**(b)** Solve the equation $3(4y + 7) - 4(5 - y) = 33$.

6. **(a)** The height, $x$ cm, of a cabin crew member for British Airways must be not less than 157.5 cm and not more than 185 cm. Express this height requirement as an inequality in $x$.

**(b)** Jennifer's height is 157 cm. Can she join the cabin crew? Explain your answer.

7. **(a)** Represent the solutions of the inequality $x > 9$ on a number line.

**(b)** State the smallest prime number that satisfies the inequality $x > 9$.

8. **(a)** Plot the points $A(-3, 1)$ and $B(5, 4)$ on the Cartesian plane. Draw the line $AB$.

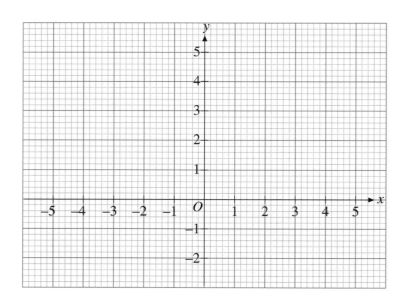

**(b)** Find the gradient of the line $AB$.

9. An arithmetic sequence is 43, 36, 29, 22, … .
   (a) State the term-to-term rule of the sequence.

   (b) Find the values of the 5th term and the 6th term.

10. The first four terms of a sequence are 7, 10, 13, 16 respectively.
    (a) Express the $n$th term of the sequence in terms of $n$.

    (b) Hence find the 15th term of the sequence.

**Section B (Structured Questions)**

11. Liam, the son of Mr and Mrs Smith, gets his first job. Mr Smith's monthly salary is £100 less than twice Liam's monthly salary. Mrs Smith's monthly salary is £2100 more than Liam's monthly salary. Let £$x$ be Liam's monthly salary.
    (a) Express the monthly salaries of Mr Smith and Mrs Smith in terms of $x$.

    (b) Express the total monthly salary of Liam and his parents in terms of $x$.

    (c) If the total monthly salary is £12 000, find Liam's monthly salary.

**12. (a)** A function $y$ of $x$ is $y = 3 - 2x$. Complete the table.

| $x$ | $-3$ | $-1$ | $2$ | $4$ |
|---|---|---|---|---|
| $y$ | 9 | 5 | $-1$ | $-5$ |

**(b)** Draw the graph of $y = 3 - 2x$ on the Cartesian plane.

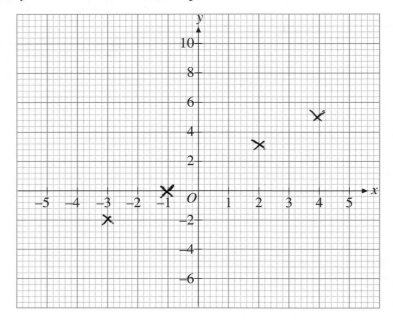

**(c)** State the coordinates of the point where the graph cuts the $x$-axis.

$(-1, 0)$

**13.** The temperature, $T\,°C$, at an altitude $x$ km above sea level is given by the function $T = 24 - 6x$.

   **(a)** Complete the table of values of $x$ and $T$.

| $x$ | 0 | 2 | 4 | 6 | 8 |
|-----|---|---|---|---|---|
| $T$ | ~~18~~ 24 | ~~16~~ 12 | ~~14~~ 0 | ~~12~~ -12 | ~~10~~ -24 |

   **(b)** Using the scale of 1 cm to 1 unit on the $x$-axis and 1 cm to 5 units on the $T$-axis, draw the graph of $T = 24 - 6x$ for $0 \leqslant x \leqslant 8$.

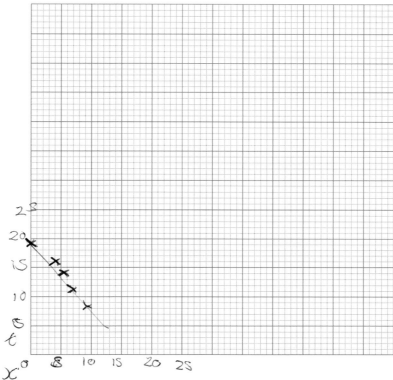

   **(c)** Using the graph, find the altitude at which the temperature is $-3\,°C$.

   $- 3 \cdot 5$

   **(d)** State the gradient of the graph and interpret its meaning in this function.

   $- 1 \cdot 5$

**14.** A rope is 2430 cm long. One-third of the rope is cut off. One-third of the remaining length is then cut off. This is repeated with one-third of the remaining length being cut off each time. Let $T_n$ cm be the length of the remaining rope after the $n$th cut.

(a) Find $T_1$, $T_2$, $T_3$ and $T_4$.

(b) Show that $T_1$, $T_2$, $T_3$, $T_4$, ... is a geometric sequence.

(c) Express $T_n$ in terms of $n$.

**15.** Maira uses sticks of lengths 13 cm and 8 cm to form a sequence of triangular frames as shown. Let $L_n$ cm be the total length of the sticks and $P_n$ cm be the perimeter of the shape formed in position number $n$.

$$13 \quad 13$$
$$8$$
$$n = 1 \qquad n = 2 \qquad n = 3$$

(a) Draw the shape for $n = 4$.

(b) Complete the table of $L_n$ and $P_n$.

| $n$ | $L_n$ | $P_n$ |
|-----|-------|-------|
| 1   |       |       |
| 2   |       |       |
| 3   |       |       |
| 4   |       |       |

(c) Express the general term $L_n$ in terms of $n$.

(d) Express the general term $P_n$ in terms of $n$.

✓ **Track your progress in the checklist on page iv.**

# Angles in Quadrilaterals and Polygons

State the geometric reasoning in your working.

## 9.1 Quadrilaterals

### LEVEL 1

1. (a) Underline the names of quadrilaterals that have four right angles.
       parallelogram   rectangle   rhombus   square   trapezium

   (b) Underline the names of quadrilaterals that have equal diagonals.
       parallelogram   rectangle   rhombus   square   trapezium

   (c) Underline the names of quadrilaterals that have equal sides.
       parallelogram   rectangle   rhombus   square   trapezium

2. (a) *ABCD* is a parallelogram.
       Find the unknowns $x$ and $y$.

   (b) *EFGH* is a rectangle.
       Find the unknowns $x$ and $y$.

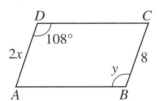

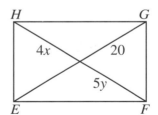

3. (a) *KLMN* is a rhombus.
       Find the unknowns $x$ and $y$.

   (b) *PQRS* is a square.
       Find the unknowns $x$ and $y$.

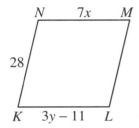

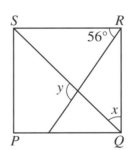

**4.** *ABCD* is a parallelogram. Find the angles *x* and *y*.

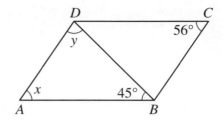

**5.** *EFGH* is a rectangle. Find the angles *x*, *y* and *z*.

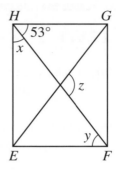

**6.** *KLMN* is a rhombus. Find the angles *x*, *y* and *z*.

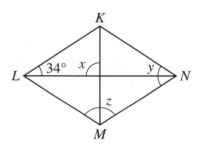

**7.** *PQRS* is a square. *PT* = 24 cm and *ST* = 3*y* cm. Find
   **(a)** the length of *PR*,

   **(b)** the value of *y*,

   **(c)** the angle *x*.

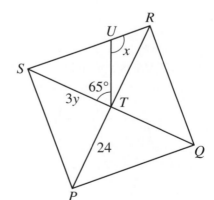

**8.** The diagram shows a 2D figure in which *ABCE* is a rhombus and *CDE* is an equilateral triangle.

(a) Show that *AE = DE*.

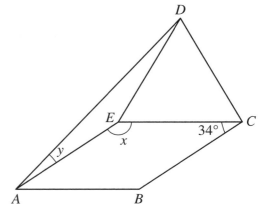

(b) Find the angle *x*.

(c) Find the angle *y*.

**9.** The diagram shows a 2D figure in which *ABCD* is a rhombus and *ABEF* is a parallelogram.

(a) Show that *BC = EF*.

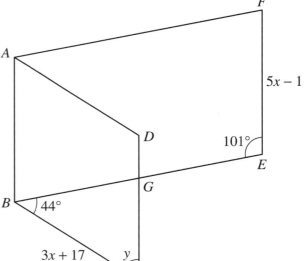

(b) *BC* = (3*x* + 17) cm and *EF* = (5*x* − 1) cm. Find the length of *AB*.

(c) Calculate the angle *y*.

# 9.2 Polygons

## LEVEL 1

1. Find the unknown angle $x$ in each polygon.
   **(a)**

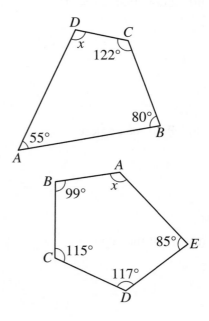

   **(b)**

2. Find the sum of the interior angles of each of these polygons.
   **(a)** Heptagon (7-gon)                    **(b)** 15-gon

3. Find the unknown angle $y$ in this diagram.

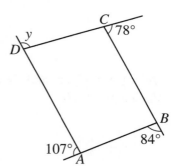

4. Find the size of each interior angle of these regular polygons.
   **(a)** Nonagon (9-gon)                    **(b)** Dodecagon (12-gon)

**5.** Find the unknown angle $x$ in the polygon.

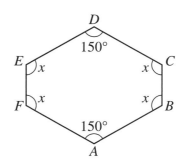

**6.** *PQRST* is a pentagon with *QP // RS*. Find angles $x$ and $y$.

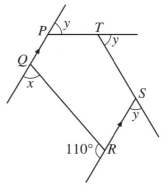

**7.** Each exterior angle of a polygon is 18°. Find the number of sides of the polygon.

**8.** Each interior angle of a polygon is 160°. Find the number of sides of the polygon.

**9.** *ABCDEF* is a regular hexagon and *BGHKC* is a regular pentagon. Find
 **(a)** ∠*KCD*,

 **(b)** ∠*CKD*.

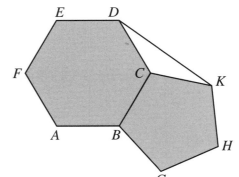

**10.** **(a)** Draw the lines of symmetry on the regular octagonal plate in the photograph.

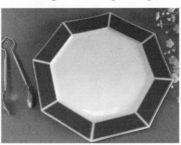

**(b)** *ABCD* is a quadrilateral bounded by four identical regular octagons. What kind of quadrilateral is *ABCD*? Explain your answer.

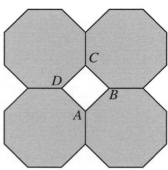

**11.** *ABCDEFGHIJ* is a regular decagon.

**(a)** State the number of lines of symmetry of a regular decagon.

**(b)** State the order of rotation symmetry of a regular decagon.

**(c)** Find all of the interior angles of △*CDE*.

**(d)** Find all of the interior angles of △*OFG*.

## 10.1 Area of Parallelograms

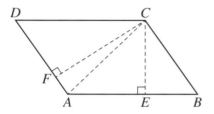

**LEVEL 1**

**1.** Identify the height corresponding to the base *BC* in each parallelogram.

**(a)**

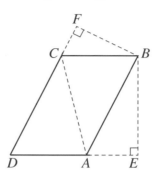

Circle one of: *AC* *EC* *FC*

**(b)**

Circle one of: *AC* *EB* *CF*

**2.** Calculate the area of the parallelogram *ABCD*, where the unit of length is cm.

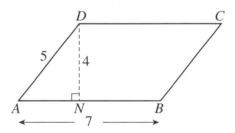

**3.** Calculate the area of the parallelogram *KLMN*, where the unit of length is cm.

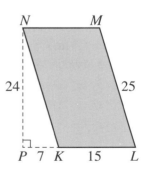

**4.** Calculate the area of the parallelogram *TXYZ*, where the lengths are in metres.

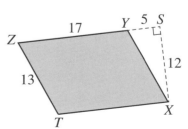

5. *ABCD* is a parallelogram. $BC = 8$ cm, $CD = 9$ cm and $DN = 6$ cm. Calculate
   (a) the area of *ABCD*,

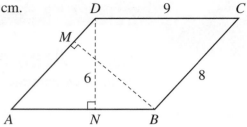

   (b) the length of *BM*.

6. *ABCD* and *EFGH* are two parallelograms between the parallel lines *ADEH* and *BCFG*. $AD = 18$ cm, $EH = 12$ cm and the area of *EFGH* is $288$ cm$^2$.
   (a) Calculate the area of *ABCD*.

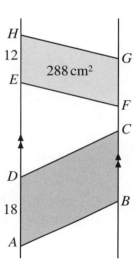

288 cm²

   (b) Is the ratio of the area of *ABCD* to the area of *EFGH* equal to $AD:EH$? Explain your answer.

7. *PQRS* is a field in the shape of a rhombus. $PQ = 37$ m, $PR = 70$ m and $QS = 24$ m. Calculate
   (a) the area of *PQRS*,

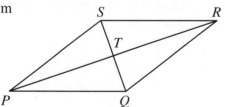

   (b) the perpendicular height from *S* to *PQ*.

8.  A garden designer plans to build a path across a rectangular lawn *TXYZ*, where *XY* = 8 m. One design is a rectangle *ABCD* with *AB* = 2 m. Another design is a parallelogram *PQRS* with *PQ* = 2 m and *PS* = 10 m.

    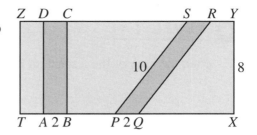

    (a)  Are the areas of *ABCD* and *PQRS* equal? Explain your answer.

    (b)  Are the perimeters of *ABCD* and *PQRS* equal? Explain your answer.

9.  *ABCD* is a parallelogram. *M* is the midpoint of *AB*. *N* is the midpoint of *DC*. The area of △*BCM* is 6 cm².

    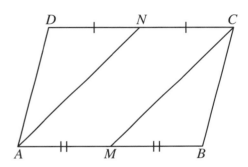

    (a)  (i)  What is the area of *ABCD*? Explain your answer.

        (ii)  Find the area of *AMCN*.

    (b)  If *AB* = 6 cm, find the perpendicular height from *C* to *AB*.

10.  An architect is designing a handrail along a staircase. Each vertical bar is 60 cm long. The distance between adjacent vertical bars is 30 cm. Calculate

    (a)  the area of *ABKL*,

    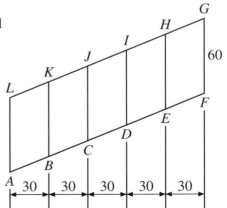

    (b)  the ratio of the area of *ADIL* to the area of *DFGI*.

# 10.2   Area of Trapezia

## ⚙ LEVEL 1

1.   Find the area of the trapezium *ABCD*, where the lengths are in cm.

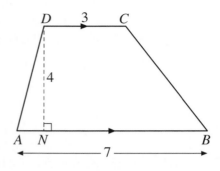

2.   Find the area of the trapezium *EFGH*, where the lengths are in metres.

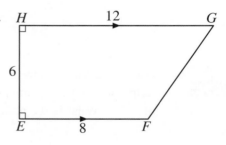

3.   Find the area of the trapezium *PQRS*, where the lengths are in metres.

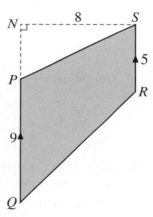

4.   Find the area of the trapezium *TXYZ*, where the lengths are in cm.

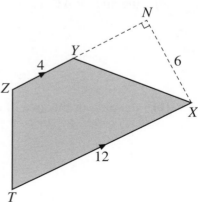

5.  *KLMN* is a trapezium. *KL* = 5 cm, *NM* = 14 cm and the area of *KLMN* is 57 cm². Find the length of *MP*.

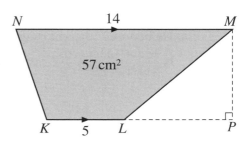

6.  *ABCD* is a parallelogram. *M* is the midpoint of *AB* and *N* is a point on *DC*. *DN* = 8 cm and *NC* = 4 cm.
    **(a)** Find the ratio of the area of *AMND* to the area of *MBCN*.

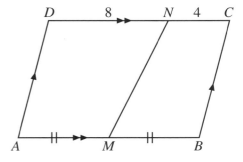

    **(b)** If the area of *ABCD* is 96 cm², find the area of *MBCN*.

7.  *PQRS* is a trapezium with *PQ* = 25 cm and *SR* = 16 cm. The area of △*QRS* = 160 cm². Calculate
    **(a)** the length of *QT*,

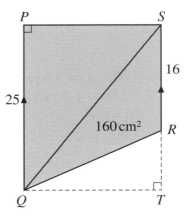

    **(b)** the area of *PQRS*.

8. *AD*, *BE* and *CF* are three parallel rungs on a ladder. The vertical distance between adjacent rungs is the same.

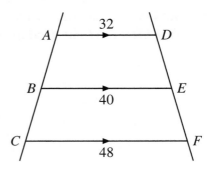

   (a) Is $\dfrac{\text{area of } ABED}{\text{area of } BCFE} = \dfrac{AD}{CF}$? Justify your answer.

   (b) If the area of *ABED* is 612 cm², find the area of *BCFE*.

9. *ABCD* is a square plot of land of sides 60 m. It is divided into three parts of equal area by the line segments *CN*, *DN* and *MN*.

   (a) Show that *M* is the midpoint of *AB*.

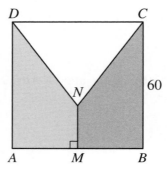

   (b) Find the length of *MN*.

10. *T* is a point on the side *SP* of a parallelogram *PQRS*. Side *QR* = 15 cm, *NQ* = 12 cm and the area of *QRST* is 126 cm². Calculate

    (a) the length of *TS*,

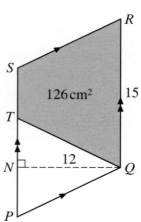

    (b) the area of △*PQT* as a percentage of the area of *PQRS*.

# 10.3   Perimeter and Area of Composite Plane Figures

## ⚙ LEVEL 1

1.  $QRST$ is a parallelogram and $QTN$ is a straight line. $PQ = 15\,cm$,
    $QR = 6\,cm$, $RS = 17\,cm$, $SN = 4\,cm$ and $TP = 8\,cm$. Find
    (a)   the perimeter of $PQRST$,

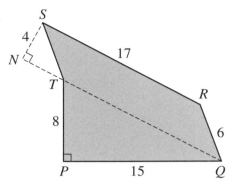

    (b)   the area of $PQRST$.

2.  The figure $ABCDEF$ is the cross-section of a house. $ABCF$ is a
    rectangle and $CDEF$ is a trapezium. $AB = 6\,m$, $BC = 2\,m$,
    $ED = 4\,m$ and $EN = 1.5\,m$. Calculate the area of $ABCDEF$.

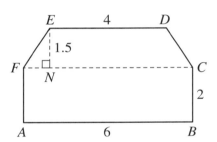

3.  This shape is formed by cutting out the semicircle $BEF$ from the
    parallelogram $ABCD$. $BC = 29\,cm$, $CD = 60\,cm$ and $DG = 20\,cm$.
    The radius of the semicircle is $15\,cm$. Find, in terms of $\pi$,
    (a)   the perimeter of the shape,

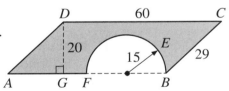

    (b)   the area of the shape.

4.  The shape *ABCDEFG* is formed by a trapezium *ABCG*, a rectangle *CDFG* and a semicircle *DEF*. The base *AB* = 8 cm, the height from *AB* to *GC* is 6 cm and *CD* = 2 cm. The radius of the semicircle is 2 cm.
    Calculate the area of the shape, giving your answer to the nearest cm².

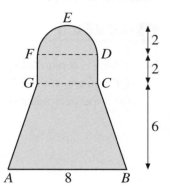

5.  *BCDE* is a square of area 169 cm². *ABEF* is a parallelogram with *AB* = 15 cm and *EN* = 12 cm. Find
    **(a)** the length of *CD*,

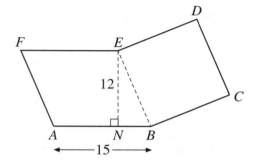

    **(b)** the perimeter of the shape *ABCDEF*,

    **(c)** the area of the shape *ABCDEF*.

6.  The symmetrical shape shown is the cross-section of a container. The shape is formed of two trapezia, *ABCK* and *CDHK*, joined at *CK* with a semicircle *EFG* cut out.
    *AB* = 16 cm, *KC* = 8 cm and *HD* = 12 cm. The height from *C* to *AB* is 2 cm. The height from *C* to *HD* is 4 cm. The radius of the semicircle is 3 cm.
    Work out the area of the shape, giving your answer to three significant figures.

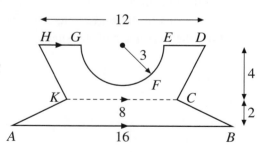

**7.** The unit of length in the diagram is cm. The area of *QRST* is 972 cm². Find
    **(a)** the length of *QT*,

    **(b)** the area of the shape *PQRST*.

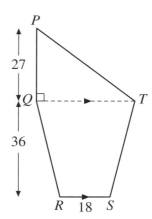

**8.** The shape shown is formed by a quarter of a circle with centre *O*, and two parallelograms *OPQV* and *OVRS*. The radius of the circle is 14 cm. *PQ* = *SR* = 20 cm and *QV* = *RV* = 28 cm. The perpendicular heights from *P* and *S* to *OV* are both 20 cm.

Using $\pi = \dfrac{22}{7}$, calculate

    **(a)** the perimeter of the shape,

    **(b)** the area of the shape.

**9.** In the diagram, *ABFM* is a rectangle, *CDEF* is a parallelogram and *HGLK* is a trapezium. All lengths are in cm. The area of *HGLK* is 54 cm². Calculate
    **(a)** the perimeter of the shaded shape,

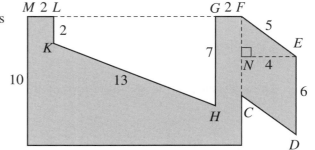

    **(b)** the area of the shaded shape.

# Volume and Surface Area of Prisms and Cylinders

## 11.1 Views and Nets of Three-dimensional (3D) Shapes

### LEVEL 1

1. Draw a sketch of each shape.

   (a)

   (b)

2. Draw the plan and the front elevation of this 3D shape.

   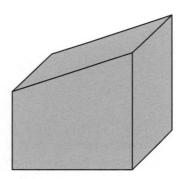

   Plan                          Front elevation

3. Draw a sketch of the 3D shape formed by this net.

   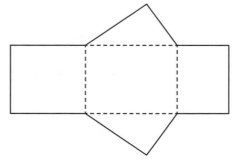

**4.** Explain whether or not the given shape can be a view of
(a) a triangular prism,

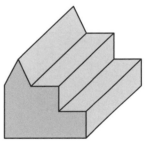

(b) a cylinder.

**5.** Draw the plan, the front elevation and the side elevation from the right of this solid.

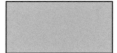

Plan                                          Front elevation

Side elevation from the right

**6.** Draw a net of this solid.

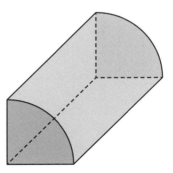

**7.** Sketch two different views of this vase.

View 1                    View 2

 **8.** Sketch the shape of a possible solid that has the given views.

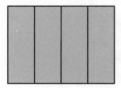

Plan

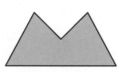

Front elevation

 **9.** Complete the net of a triangular prism.

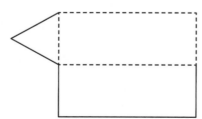

# 11.2 Volume and Total Surface Area of Prisms

**1.** The diagram shows a triangular prism. $AB = 17\,$cm, $BC = 15\,$cm, $CA = 8\,$cm, $BE = 24\,$cm and $\angle ACB = 90°$. Calculate

    **(a)** the volume of the prism,

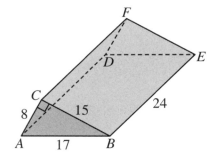

    **(b)** the total surface area of the prism.

**2.** The diagram shows a trapezoidal prism. All lengths are in cm. Find

    **(a)** the volume of the prism,

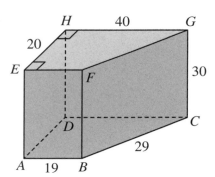

    **(b)** the total surface area of the prism.

**3.** The diagram shows a prism whose cross-section is a parallelogram $ABCD$. $AD = 41\,$cm, $DN = 40\,$cm, $HG = 30\,$cm and $BF = 36\,$cm. Work out

    **(a)** the volume of the prism,

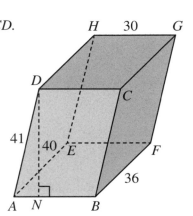

    **(b)** the total surface area of the prism.

**4.** The diagram shows an L-shaped prism. All angles in *ABCDEF* are right angles. *AB* = 8 cm, *BC* = 12 cm, *RS* = 4 cm, *UP* = 5 cm and *PA* = 6 cm. Find

    **(a)** the area of *ABCDEF*,

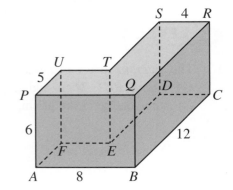

    **(b)** the volume of the prism.

**5.** The diagram shows a pentagonal prism. *AB* = *EA* = 6 cm, *BC* = *DE* = 5 cm and *CD* = 4 cm. The area of *ABCDE* is 46 cm². The volume of the prism is 276 cm³. Calculate

    **(a)** the length of *DS*,

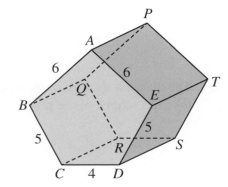

    **(b)** the total surface area of the prism.

**6.** The diagram shows a trapezoidal prism. *AB* = 22 cm, *BC* = 24 cm, *CD* = 12 cm and *DA* = 26 cm. The volume of the prism is 12 240 cm³. Calculate

    **(a)** the area of *ABCD*,

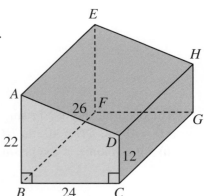

    **(b)** the length of *CG*,

    **(c)** the total surface area of the prism.

7.  The diagram shows a trough. It is a triangular prism, open at the top.
    $AB = CB = 34\,$cm, $NB = 30\,$cm and $AD = 50\,$cm. The area of
    $\triangle ABC = 480\,$cm$^2$. Calculate

    (a)  the length of $AC$,

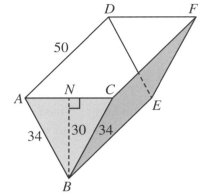

    (b)  the volume of the trough,

    (c)  the external surface area of the trough.

8.  A vaulting box can be modelled by a trapezoidal prism as shown. $AD = BC = 111\,$cm, $CD = 30\,$cm,
    $DN = 105\,$cm and $BF = 140\,$cm. The area of $ABCD = 6930\,$cm$^2$.

    Find
    (a)  the length of $AB$,

    (b)  the volume of the prism,

    (c)  the surface area of the prism, excluding the face $ABFE$.

# 11.3 Volume and Total Surface Area of Cylinders

Use the value of $\pi$ from your calculator and give your answers to three significant figures unless stated otherwise.

## ⚙ LEVEL 1

1. A cylinder has a base radius of 1 cm and a height of 2.5 cm.
   (a) Draw a net of the cylinder.

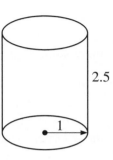

2.5

1

   (b) Find the volume of the cylinder.

   (c) Find the total surface area of the cylinder.

2. A cylindrical can has a base radius of 4 cm and a height of 10 cm. Calculate
   (a) its volume,

   (b) its total surface area.

3. A cylindrical open-topped tank has a diameter of 4 m and a height of 3 m. Calculate its external surface area.

4. A cylinder has a base radius of 5 cm. Its volume is $150\pi\,\text{cm}^3$. Calculate
   (a) the height of the cylinder,

   (b) the total surface area of the cylinder, in terms of $\pi$.

5. A cylinder has a base radius of 7 cm. Its surface area is $252\pi\,\text{cm}^2$. Work out
   (a) the height of the cylinder,

   (b) the volume of the cylinder, in terms of $\pi$.

6. The uniform cross-section of a bar is a quarter of a circle of radius 6 cm. The length of the bar is 13 cm. Calculate
   (a) the volume of the bar,

   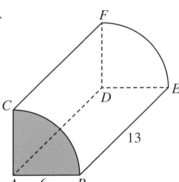

   (b) the total surface area of the bar.

**7.** The roller of a road compactor is a cylinder which has a diameter of 1 m and a width of 1.4 m. Calculate

    **(a)** the volume of the roller,

    **(b)** the area of the road that the roller presses when it rotates fully 10 times.

**8.** A measuring cylinder of base diameter 6 cm has some water in it. When a solid metal ball is submerged into the water, the water level rises by 2 cm. Work out the volume of the ball.

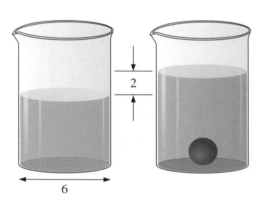

**9.** A solid metal disc has a base radius of 10 cm and a height of 6 cm. It is melted and recast into cylinders, each of base radius 2 cm and height 5 cm.

    **(a)** How many cylinders can be made?

    **(b)** Find the ratio of the surface area of the disc to the total surface area of all the cylinders formed.

☑ **Track your progress in the checklist on page iv.**

# 11.4　Volume and Surface Area of Composite Solids

Use the value of $\pi$ from your calculator and give your answers to three significant figures unless stated otherwise.

⚙ **LEVEL 1**

**1.**　Convert $20\,\text{cm}^2$ to $\text{m}^2$.

**2.**　Convert $5\,\text{m}^2$ to $\text{cm}^2$.

**3.**　Express $4500\,\text{cm}^3$ in $\text{m}^3$.

**4.**　Express $3\,\text{m}^3$ in $\text{cm}^3$.

**5.**　The cross-section of a prism consists of a rectangle and a trapezium. The lengths shown are in cm. Find
　　**(a)**　the volume of the prism,

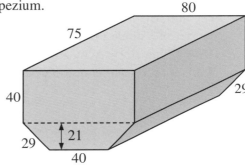

　　**(b)**　the total surface area of the prism.

**6.**　*ABCDEF* is the end face of a prism, formed by two identical parallelograms *ABEF* and *BCDE*. *AB* = 13 cm, *AF* = 30 cm, the perpendicular distance between *AF* and *BE* = 12 cm and *CR* = 54 cm.
　　Work out
　　**(a)**　the volume of the prism,

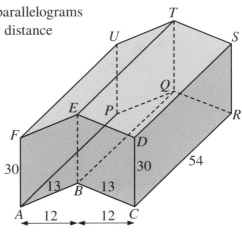

　　**(b)**　the total surface area of the prism.

**7.** The diagram shows a trinket box. Its body is a cuboid 30 cm long, 20 cm wide and 16 cm high. Its lid has a semicircular uniform cross-section of radius 10 cm. Find

    **(a)** the total external surface area of the box,

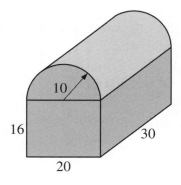

    **(b)** the volume of the box.

**8.** The uniform cross-section of a door wedge consists of a quarter of a circle joined to a right-angled triangle. $AB = 12$ cm, $BD = 5$ cm, $AD = 13$ cm and $CG = 6$ cm. Work out the volume of the wedge.

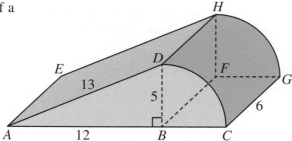

**9.** The solid shown is formed by two cylinders. The top cylinder has a base radius of 2 cm and a height of 6 cm. The bottom cylinder has a base radius of 5 cm and a height of 4 cm. Calculate, in terms of $\pi$,

    **(a)** the total surface area of the composite solid,

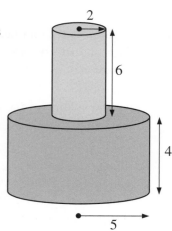

    **(b)** the volume of the solid.

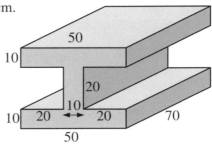

**10.** The diagram shows an H-shaped iron girder. The unit of length is cm.

    **(a)** Calculate the total surface area of the girder.

    **(b)** The density of iron is 7.86 g/cm³. Find the mass of the girder in grams.

**11.** The uniform cross-section of a concrete road block is shown in the diagram on the right. It consists of two trapezia above a rectangle. The unit of length is cm.

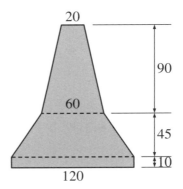

    **(a)** Find the area of the cross-section

        **(i)** in cm²,

        **(ii)** in m².

    **(b)** The length of the road block is 2 m. Find the volume of the road block

        **(i)** in cm³,

        **(ii)** in m³.

## 12.1 Line Graphs

### ⚙ LEVEL 1

**1.** A cup of hot water is placed on a table to cool. The line graph shows the temperature of the water over the next 60 minutes.

    **(a)** What is the initial temperature of the water?

    **(b)** Describe the change of the water temperature.

    **(c)** At what time does the water temperature reach 24 °C?

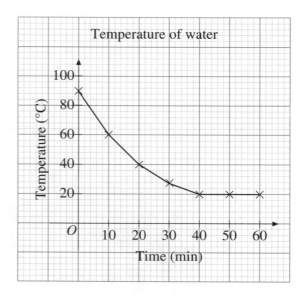

**2.** Tom represents his heart rate during an exercise period in the line graph.

    **(a)** What is his heart rate before exercising?

    **(b)** Describe the trend of his heart rate.

    **(c)** After how many minutes does his heart rate exceed 100 beats/min?

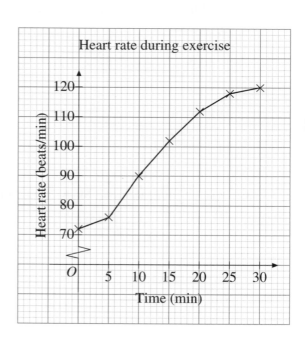

**FINANCE**

**3.** The line graph shows the price of a hotel room per night between June and October.

(a) What is the highest price? In which month does it occur?

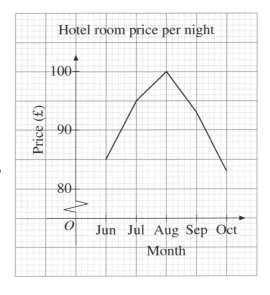

(b) In which months is the price lower than £90 per night?

**4.** The table records the height of a girl from birth to age four.

| Age (years) | 0 | 1 | 2 | 3 | 4 |
|---|---|---|---|---|---|
| Height (cm) | 52 | 74 | 85 | 95 | 103 |

(a) Draw a line graph to display the data.

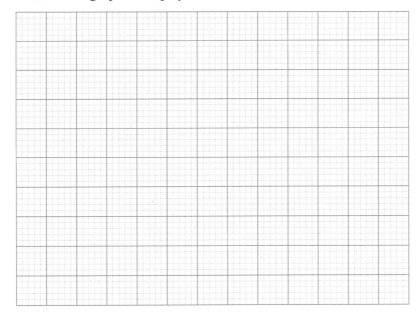

(b) When was the girl taller than 90 cm?

(c) Use the graph to estimate the height of the girl when she is five years old.

SCIENCE

**5.** The table shows the tide level of the River Thames at London Bridge on 18 March 2018.

| Time | 00:00 | 03:00 | 06:00 | 09:00 | 12:00 | 15:00 | 18:00 | 21:00 | 24:00 |
|---|---|---|---|---|---|---|---|---|---|
| Height (m) | 4.9 | 6.6 | 2.9 | 0.5 | 4.2 | 6.9 | 3.2 | 0.8 | 4.2 |

**(a)** Display the data on a line graph.

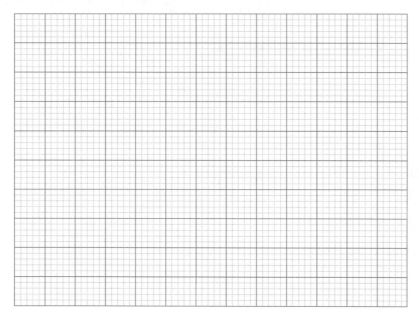

**(b)** From the graph, find the time intervals during which the height of the tide was over 5 m.

**(c)** Describe the pattern of the tide level on that day.

**6.** The table shows the number of visitors to the UK from 2007 to 2016.

| Year | 2007 | 2008 | 2009 | 2010 | 2011 | 2012 | 2013 | 2014 | 2015 | 2016 |
|---|---|---|---|---|---|---|---|---|---|---|
| **Number of visitors (thousands)** | 32 778 | 31 888 | 29 886 | 29 804 | 30 798 | 31 085 | 32 689 | 34 380 | 36 114 | 37 610 |

**(a)** Represent the data in a line graph.

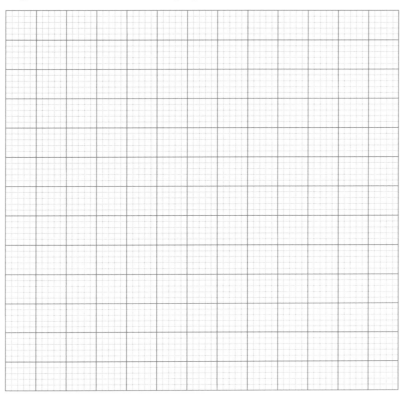

**(b)** Describe the trend of the data.

**(c)** Calculate the percentage increase in the number of visitors from 2015 to 2016. Give your answer to the nearest 1%.

**(d)** Use the graph to estimate the number of visitors in 2017. Give your answer to the nearest 1000.

# 12.2 Pie Charts

### ⚙ LEVEL 1

1. The pie chart shows the proportion of participants in a swimming gala who swam in the different styles.

   (a) Which swimming style had the greatest number of participants?

   (b) Find the ratio of the number of freestyle swimmers to the number of backstroke swimmers.

Participants in a swimming gala

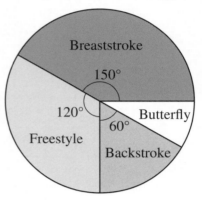

2. The pie chart displays the sales of three brands of yoghurt, Healthy, Happy and Smoothy.

   (a) Find the value of $x$.

   (b) Calculate the sales of Healthy yoghurt as a percentage of the total sales of the three brands.

Sales of three brands of yoghurt

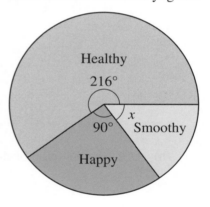

3. The numbers in the pie chart represent the numbers of students at a language school who are learning each second language.

   (a) Calculate the angle of the sector for German.

   (b) Find the percentage of students at the school who are learning French.

Second language of students

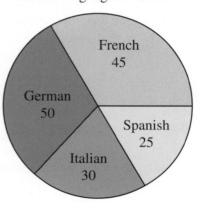

**4.** A question in a questionnaire asks the age of the respondents. A respondent can choose age brackets A, B, C or D. The percentages of respondents choosing A, B and C are shown. 140 people chose C.

| A | B | C | D |
|---|---|---|---|
| 30% | 35% | 25% | |

**(a)** How many people chose D?

**(b)** Draw a pie chart to represent the data.

**5.** The table shows the percentages of types of households by size in the UK in 2017.

| Type of household | One person | Two people | Three people | Four or more people |
|---|---|---|---|---|
| **Percentage** | 28% | 35% | 16% | 21% |

**(a)** The data is represented by this pie chart. Label the pie chart.

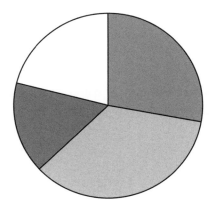

**(b)** Calculate the angle of the sector for households with two people.

£ **6.** The pie chart shows the total spending of the UK in the financial year 2018.

UK total spending 2018

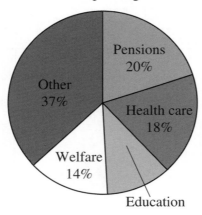

**(a)** What is the percentage of spending on education?

**(b)** What is the angle of the sector for pensions?

**(c)** Find the ratio of spending on health care to spending on welfare.

**7.** The pie chart shows the sales of batteries A, B, C and D in a shop.
**(a)** Find the sales of type C batteries as a percentage of the total number of batteries sold.

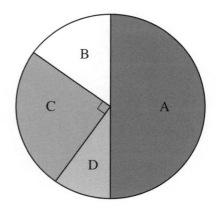

**(b)** Make one comparison of the sales of type A batteries with the sales of the other types of batteries.

**(c)** If 240 type C batteries were sold, what was the total number of batteries sold?

## 12.3  Use and Misuse of Statistical Graphs

⚙ **LEVEL 1**

**1.**  State which type of statistical graph is most appropriate for each data set.

   **(a)**  Populations of some countries in 2017

   | Country | Population |
   |---|---|
   | France | 64 979 548 |
   | Germany | 82 114 224 |
   | United Kingdom | 66 181 585 |
   | United States | 324 459 463 |

   **(b)**  Spending by a family

   | Category | Percentage of total spending |
   |---|---|
   | Rent | 25% |
   | Food | 30% |
   | Transport | 10% |
   | Other | 35% |

**2.**  Which type of statistical graph should be used to display this data? Explain your answers briefly.

   **(a)**  The number of students enrolled in a school each year in the last five years

   **(b)**  The percentage of votes for each candidate in a student society election

**£**
FINANCE
**3.**  The bar chart shows the sales of four types of magazine in a newsagent.

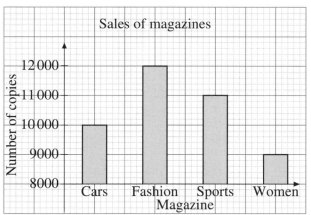

   **(a)**  Work out the ratio of the length of the bar for 'Cars' to that for 'Fashion'.

   **(b)**  The newsagent manager says that the sales of fashion magazines are twice the sales of car magazines. Is she correct? Explain your answer.

**4.** The table shows the number of members in four clubs.

| Club | Members |
|------|---------|
| Dancing | 38 |
| Rowing | 29 |
| Swimming | 25 |
| Tennis | 32 |

    **(a)** Name a suitable type of statistical graph to show

        **(i)** the number of members in each club,

        **(ii)** the proportion of the total club members in each club.

    **(b)** Is it appropriate to display the data using a line graph? Explain your answer.

**5.** The bar chart shows customers' online reviews of a restaurant.

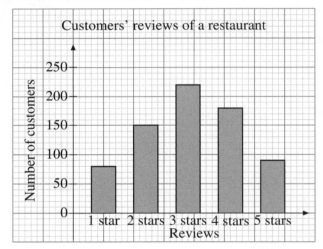

    **(a)** Represent the data using a pie chart.

    **(b)** State an advantage of showing this data in a pie chart instead of a bar chart.

£ **6.** The bar chart shows average weekly spending by children, by age group and gender, in the UK from
FINANCE    2015 to 2017.

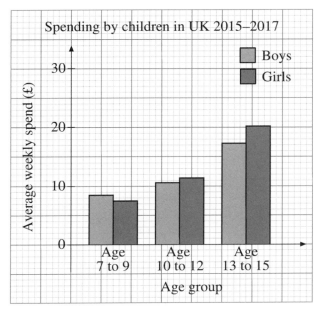

(a) In which age group is the average spending by boys higher than that by girls?

(b) What can you say about the weekly spending by a child as the child gets older?

(c) Estimate the ratio of the average spending by girls age 7 to 9 years to that by girls age 13 to 15
years. Give your answer in its simplest form.

**£ 7.** The line graph shows the sales of cars by a car dealer in four months.

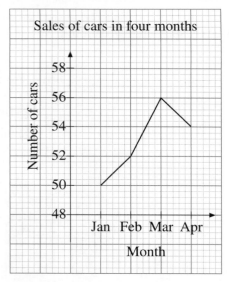

**(a)** By observing the graph, Marcus claims that the number of cars sold in March is four times the number sold in January. Do you agree with him? Explain your answer. If you disagree, what mistake do you think Marcus has made?

**(b)** Find the percentage increase in sales in March compared to the sales in January.

✓ **Track your progress in the checklist on page iv.**

# 12.4    Scatter Graphs

**1.**    **(a)**    Plot the scatter graph of $y$ against $x$ for this data.

| $x$ | 2 | 4 | 6 | 8 | 10 |
|---|---|---|---|---|---|
| $y$ | 0.4 | 2.7 | 5.3 | 7.6 | 10.2 |

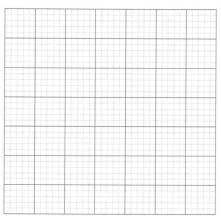

**(b)**    State whether the data shows positive correlation, negative correlation or no correlation.

**2.**    State the relationship between $x$ and $y$ in each of these scatter graphs.

**(a)** 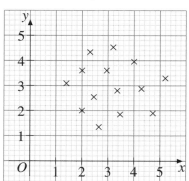    **(b)**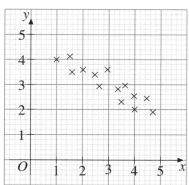

**3.**    State which of the lines A, B or C is the line of best fit
for the plotted data.

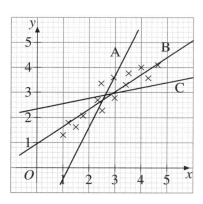

£ **4.** The scatter graph shows the prices and the performance ratings of some toasters.

FINANCE

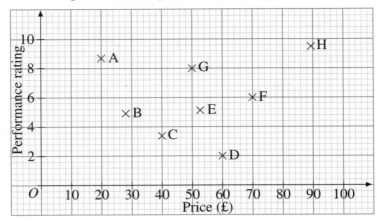

(a) What is the price of toaster G and what is its performance rating?

(b) Name a toaster that is cheaper than toaster G but has a performance rating higher than G.

(c) Name a toaster that costs more than toaster G but has a performance rating lower than G.

(d) Is there any relationship between the price and the performance rating of a toaster? Explain your answer.

**5.** The diagram shows the scatter graph for a set of data in $x$ and $y$ and its line of best fit.

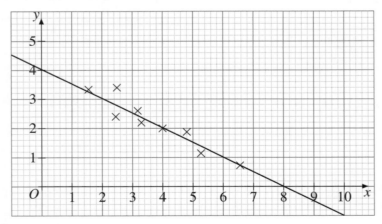

(a) State the type of correlation between $x$ and $y$.

(b) Find the equation of the line of best fit.

**(c)** Estimate the value of $y$ when $x = 5$ using the equation of the line of best fit.

6. The table shows the ages of some employees and the training hours they required to use a new software package.

| Age, $x$ (years) | 25 | 30 | 34 | 39 | 42 | 48 | 52 |
|---|---|---|---|---|---|---|---|
| Training time, $y$ (hours) | 3.0 | 3.6 | 4.0 | 4.4 | 4.8 | 5.4 | 5.7 |

**(a)** Draw a scatter graph for the data.

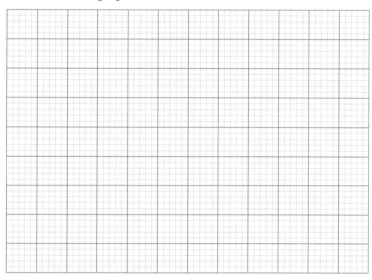

**(b)** What can you say about the relationship between the age of an employee and the training time?

**(c)** Draw a line of best fit by eye for the data.

**(d)** The training time of an employee is 4.5 hours. Use the graph of the line of best fit to estimate the age of the employee.

**7.** A student measures the thicknesses of different stacks of A4 paper and records the results.

| Number of sheets | 40 | 100 | 160 | 210 | 270 | 310 | 360 | 420 |
|---|---|---|---|---|---|---|---|---|
| Thickness (mm) | 4 | 10 | 15 | 22 | 26 | 40 | 38 | 41 |

**(a)** Complete the scatter graph of the student's results.

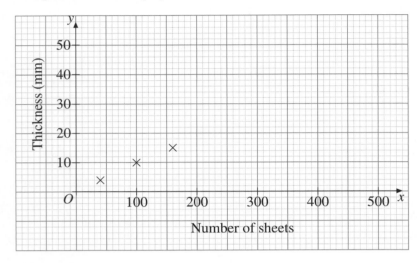

**(b)** One of the student's measurements is wrong. Circle this one on your graph.

**(c)** Draw a line of best fit on your scatter graph, excluding the incorrect measurement.

**(d)** Find the equation of your line of best fit.

**(e)** Use your line of best fit to estimate the thickness of a stack of 250 sheets.

8. The scatter graph shows the history exam results for a group of students and the number of hours they spend playing computer games per week.

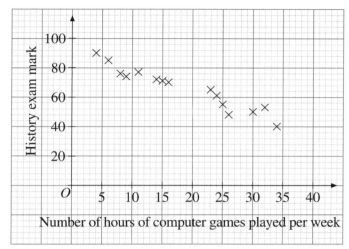

(a) What type of correlation is shown by the data?

(b) Draw a line of best fit.

(c) Find the equation of your line of best fit.

(d) A student plays 20 hours of computer games in a week. Use your line of best fit to estimate his history exam mark.

Answer all the questions. State the geometric reasoning in your working where appropriate.

**Section A (Short Questions)**

1.  *ADE* is a straight line. Find the angles *x* and *y*.

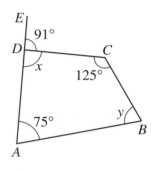

2.  The marked angles are the exterior angles of the pentagon *ABCDE*. Find the value of *x*.

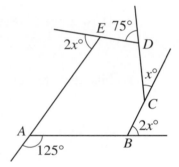

3.  *ABCD* is a rhombus. *AB* = (2*x* + 17) cm and *BC* = (5*x* − 4) cm. Find
    **(a)** the value of *x*,

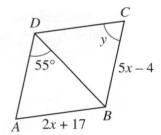

    **(b)** the perimeter of the rhombus,

    **(c)** the angle *y*.

**4.** *ABCD* is a parallelogram. *AB* = 15 cm, *AD* = 10 cm and *DN* = 9 cm. Calculate
   **(a)** the area of the parallelogram,

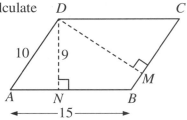

   **(b)** the length of *DM*.

**5.** *PQRS* is a trapezium. *QR* = 3 m, *RT* = 4 m and the area of *PQRS* = 18 m². Calculate the length of *PS*.

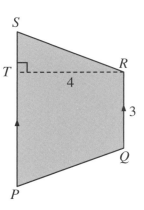

**6.** The diagram shows a copper bar that is a trapezoidal prism. *AB* = 12 cm, *BC* = *AD* = 5 cm, *DC* = 6 cm, *DN* = 4 cm and *BF* = 15 cm.
   **(a)** Find the total surface area of the bar.

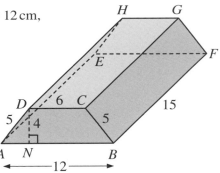

   **(b)** The density of copper is 8.9 g/cm³. Find the mass of the bar in grams.

**7.** A paint roller has a length of 30 cm and a diameter of 4 cm. Find the area painted by the roller if it makes 10 full turns in one direction. Use the value of π from your calculator and give your answer to three significant figures.

8. A carton contains 2 litres of apple juice. Olivia fills some cylindrical glasses of base radius 3 cm and a height of 12 cm. How many glasses of juice can she fill?

9. The line graph shows the average amount spent each week by children of different ages in the UK in the period 2015 to 2017.

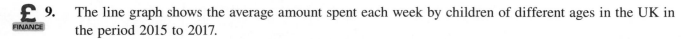

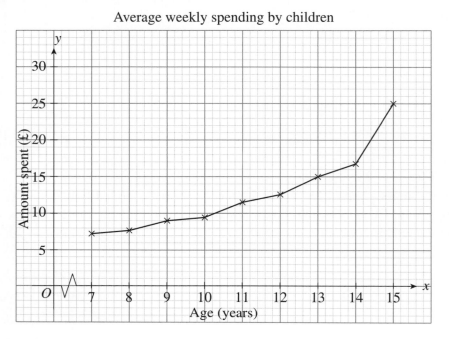

Average weekly spending by children

(a) Describe the trend of the average weekly spending by children.

(b) Express the average weekly spending at age 15 as a percentage of the average weekly spending at age 13.

**10.** The scatter graph shows the heights and femur lengths of six people.

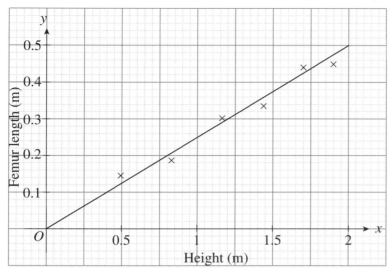

Femur length

**(a)** State the type of correlation between the height and the femur length of a person.

**(b)** Find the equation of the line of best fit shown in the diagram.

**(c)** If a person's femur length is 0.4 m, estimate the person's corresponding height from the graph.

## Section B (Structured Questions)

**11. (a)** Draw the lines of symmetry on the regular nonagon and state its order of rotation symmetry.

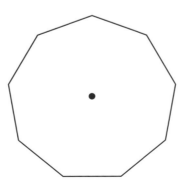

**(b)** *O* is the centre of the regular nonagon *ABCDEFGHI*. Find

    **(i)** ∠*FGH*,

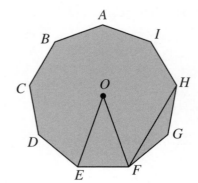

    **(ii)** ∠*EOF*,

    **(iii)** ∠*OFH*.

12. The diagram shows a symmetrical two-dimensional metal plate. *DEF* is a semicircle, *CDFG* is a square and *ABCG* is a trapezium.
    *AN* = 3 cm, *NG* = 4 cm and *GA* = 5 cm. The area of *CDFG* is 36 cm². Calculate, leaving your answers in terms of $\pi$,
    **(a)** the area of the semicircle *DEF*,

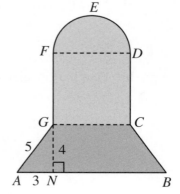

    **(b)** the area of the plate,

    **(c)** the perimeter of the plate.

**13.** The diagram shows a hut in the form of a prism. *ABE* is an isosceles triangle and *BCDE* is a rectangle. The lengths are in metres. Calculate

    **(a)** the volume of the hut,

    **(b)** the surface area of the hut, excluding the floor *CDSR*.

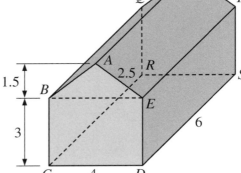

**14.** A cardboard box is tightly packed with 24 cylindrical drink cans. Each can has a diameter of 7 cm and a height of 12 cm. Work out

    **(a)** the internal surface area of the box excluding the lid flaps,

    **(b)** the volume of the box,

    **(c)** the volume of the empty space inside the box. Use the value of π from your calculator and give your answer to three significant figures.

**15.** The bar chart shows the numbers of road accident fatalities by road user type in the UK in 2016, to the nearest 10.

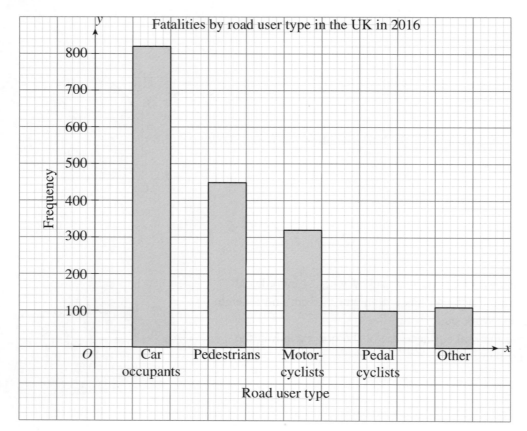

Fatalities by road user type in the UK in 2016

**(a)** Calculate the percentage of fatalities that involved pedestrians.

**(b)** Calculate the ratio of the fatalities of motorcyclists to the fatalities of pedal cyclists.

**(c)** Represent the data in a pie chart.

☑ **Track your progress in the checklist on page iv.**

# Notes